Modelling with circular motion

The School Mathematics Project

CAMBRIDGE
UNIVERSITY PRESS

Main authors	Stan Dolan
	Judith Galsworthy
	Janet Jagger
	Ann Kitchen
	Paul Roder
	Mike Savage
	Bernard Taylor
	Carole Tyler
	Nigel Webb
	Phil Wood
Team leader	Ann Kitchen
Project director	Stan Dolan

This unit has been produced in collaboration with the Mechanics in Action Project, based at the Universities of Leeds and Manchester.

The authors would like to give special thanks to Ann White for her help in producing the trial edition and in preparing this book for publication.

The publishers would like to thank the following for supplying photographs:

cover – Tick Ahearn;
page 28 – Dr Harold Edgerton/Science Photo Library;
page 73 – Mechanics in Action Project;
        UNILAB Ltd.;
page 74 – Mechanics in Action Project;
        UNILAB Ltd.;
page 75 – Mechanics in Action Project;
        UNILAB Ltd.;
page 76 – UNILAB Ltd.;
        Mechanics in Action Project.

Published by the Press Syndicate of the University of Cambridge
The Pitt Building, Trumpington Street, Cambridge CB2 1RP
40 West 20th Street, New York, NY 10011–4211, USA
10 Stamford Road, Oakleigh, Victoria 3166, Australia

© Cambridge University Press 1992

First published 1992

Cartoons by Tony Hall

Produced by Gecko Limited, Bicester, Oxon.

Cover design by Iguana Creative Design

Printed in Great Britain at the University Press, Cambridge

British Library cataloguing in publication data

A catalogue record for this book is available from the British Library.

ISBN 0 521 40889 X

Contents

1 Circular motion

1.1 Modelling horizontal circular motion

Circular motion can be fun, but is it safe? To answer this question it is necessary to analyse the forces involved.

A designer of a chair-o-plane at a fun-fair would have asked questions such as:

- Will a child swing out at a greater angle than a much heavier adult?

- Will the people on the inside swing out at the same angle as those on the outside?

- Will empty chairs be a problem?

- What will happen as the speed increases?

Although the chair-o-plane is slightly more complicated than a simple conical pendulum, analysing the motion of a conical pendulum is a sensible first step.

Tie a small mass or bob to the end of a piece of string. Set the bob moving in a horizontal circle.

(a) What forces act on the bob and on the string?

(b) Are these forces constant?

(c) What do you have to do to get small circles? How do you get large circles?

(d) What force does your hand feel? Why?

The bob of a conical pendulum performs horizontal circular motion with constant angular speed. In *Modelling with force and motion*, a mathematical analysis of circular motion yielded a number of useful results.

If a particle is rotating with a constant angular speed of ω rad s^{-1} at a distance r metres from the centre, then the velocity of the particle will have magnitude $r\omega$ m s^{-1} and its direction, although constantly changing, will always be tangential to the circle.

$$v = r\omega$$

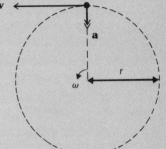

The vector acceleration of the particle will have magnitude $r\omega^2$ and its direction (again, constantly changing) will always be towards the axis of rotation.

$$a = r\omega^2 \Rightarrow a = \frac{v^2}{r}$$

Acceleration directed towards the centre of a circular motion is called **centripetal acceleration**.

Some real situations such as the chair-o-plane, the rotor and the cyclist shown in the picture at the start of the chapter lend themselves to further investigation as extended pieces of work. The chair-o-plane will be considered in the tasksheet and the other two situations can be found in exercise 1.

E X A M P L E   1

A child of mass 40 kg is sitting on a roundabout 3 metres from the central axle. The roundabout rotates at 2 rad s^{-1}. Find the resultant force acting on the child.

S O L U T I O N

Newton's second law states: resultant force = mass × acceleration
The acceleration of the child is:

$$a = r\omega^2$$
$$= 3 \times 2^2 = 12 \, \text{m s}^{-2} \text{ towards the central axle}$$
$$\Rightarrow \text{ resultant force} = 40 \times 12 = 480 \text{ newtons towards the central axle}$$

T A S K S H E E T   1   —   The chair-o-plane (page 10)

EXAMPLE 2

A penny is placed on a turntable 0.12 metre from the axis of rotation. A second penny is placed on the turntable so that its speed is half that of the first penny. The first penny starts to slide when the angular speed reaches $4\,\text{rad}\,\text{s}^{-1}$.

(a) How far from the axis of rotation is the second penny?

(b) At what angular speed would the second penny start to slide?

SOLUTION

(a) The penny is modelled as a particle of mass m rotating with angular speed ω, distance r from the axis of rotation.

The speed of the first penny is $v = \omega r$.

The speed of the second penny is $\dfrac{v}{2}$ or $\omega\left(\dfrac{r}{2}\right)$, so it must be placed a distance 0.06 metre from the axis of rotation.

(b) There are just two forces acting on the first penny, gravity and a contact force. The contact force has two components, the normal contact force, N, and friction, F.

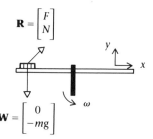

The penny has acceleration $\begin{bmatrix} r\omega^2 \\ 0 \end{bmatrix}$.

By Newton's second law: $\begin{bmatrix} 0 \\ -mg \end{bmatrix} + \begin{bmatrix} F \\ N \end{bmatrix} = m\begin{bmatrix} r\omega^2 \\ 0 \end{bmatrix}$

Therefore $F = mr\omega^2$

As the angular speed increases, friction will increase in magnitude until it reaches a limit (**limiting friction**), at which point the penny will start to slide.

The first penny starts to slide when $\omega = 4\,\text{rad}\,\text{s}^{-1}$ so limiting friction is $(0.12 \times 4^2)m = 1.92m$ newtons

Assume that limiting friction will be the same for the second penny.

$$1.92m = 0.06\,m\omega^2$$
$$\Rightarrow \qquad \omega = 5.66\,\text{rad}\,\text{s}^{-1}$$

The second penny will start to slide when the angular speed reaches $5.66\,\text{rad}\,\text{s}^{-1}$.

EXERCISE 1

Take $g = 9.8\,N\,kg^{-1}$ where necessary.

1 A racing car is travelling at a constant speed of $120\,km\,h^{-1}$ round a circular bend. The centripetal acceleration is $30\,m\,s^{-2}$. What is the radius of the bend?

2 A conical pendulum has length 80 cm and a bob of mass 0.5 kg, which is rotating in a horizontal circle of radius 30 cm. Find the angle between the string and the vertical, the tension in the string and the linear speed of the bob.

3 A thin string of length 1 metre has a breaking strain of 60 newtons. A mass of 4 kg is attached to one end and made to rotate as a conical pendulum. Draw diagrams and form an equation to describe the motion. Hence find the largest angular speed that can be attained and the angle the string makes with the vertical in this case.

4 A fairground machine consists of a large hollow cylinder of internal radius 5 metres. This can be made to rotate about its axis and a floor can be raised or lowered. When stationary, a door opens to allow a man of mass 75 kg to enter and then closes flush with the wall. The cylinder rotates faster and faster until the friction between the man's back and the wall is equal to his weight. Then the floor drops away.

Draw a force diagram showing **W** (weight), **F** (friction) and **N** (normal reaction) acting on the man. Given that the magnitude of **F** is two-fifths that of **N**, write down a vector equation and hence find the angular speed of the cylinder.

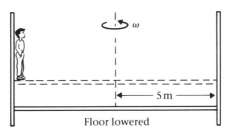

Floor lowered

5 Given below is a force diagram modelling a cyclist rounding a bend of radius 10 metres. The road is banked at an angle of 30°. The total mass of the cyclist and the bicycle is 100 kg. The speed of the cyclist is such that there is no frictional force acting sideways on the cycle tyres up or down the slope. Find the speed of the cyclist.

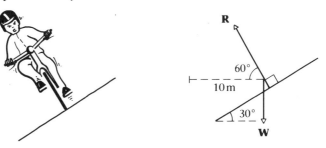

1.2 Investigating vertical circular motion

Fairground rides are designed to be safe. An engineer will formulate a mathematical model of a ride, analyse the model and then validate that the ride is safe by simulating it under laboratory conditions.

(a) Discuss the different possibilities for the motion of the marble released at the start of the loop-the-loop shown above.

(b) Set up a track to validate your answers to (a). What is the main difference between vertical and horizontal circular motion?

Newton's laws of motion and *Modelling with force and motion* dealt with many of the concepts needed to analyse motion. The further concepts of **work** and **energy**, which you will need to analyse examples of vertical circular motion, form the central theme of this unit. The aim is to show you some of the mathematical techniques associated with these concepts so that you can use them with confidence when formulating a mathematical model to describe situations such as those shown above.

After working through this chapter you should:

1   know that the acceleration directed towards the centre of circular motion is called centripetal acceleration;

2   know how to set up, analyse and interpret a mathematical model for horizontal circular motion where more than one force is acting on a body travelling with constant angular speed;

3   appreciate that many instances of circular motion do not involve constant angular speed.

The chair-o-plane

The first question a design engineer must ask is, 'Will a child swing out at a greater angle than a much heavier adult?'. Some insight into the problem can be gained by simplifying the situation and asking a similar question about the conical pendulum.

 Problem

Does a heavy bob swing out at the same angle as a light bob if they are both rotating at the same angular speed?

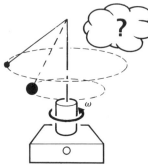

Set up a model

Assume that the bob may be modelled by a particle of mass m, distance r from the axis of rotation. The angular speed of the bob is a constant ω radians per second and the bob swings out at an angle θ radians to the vertical when the length of the string is l. You can also assume that air resistance is negligible so that there are just two forces acting on the bob, weight, **W**, and the tension in the string, **T**.

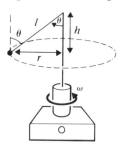

$$\mathbf{T} = \begin{bmatrix} T\sin\theta \\ T\cos\theta \end{bmatrix}$$

$$\mathbf{W} = \begin{bmatrix} 0 \\ -mg \end{bmatrix}$$

Analyse the problem

Resolving forces horizontally and vertically and adding the forces to obtain the resultant, Newton's second law gives:

$$\begin{bmatrix} T\sin\theta \\ T\cos\theta \end{bmatrix} + \begin{bmatrix} 0 \\ -mg \end{bmatrix} = \begin{bmatrix} mr\omega^2 \\ 0 \end{bmatrix}$$

$\Rightarrow T\sin\theta = mr\omega^2$ and $T\cos\theta = mg$

But $\quad r = l\sin\theta \Rightarrow T\sin\theta = ml\omega^2 \sin\theta$

$\Rightarrow \quad T = ml\omega^2$ or $\sin\theta = 0$ (i.e. $\theta = 0$)

---

1 Show that for $\theta > 0$, $\cos\theta = \dfrac{g}{l\omega^2}$

TASKSHEET **1**

Interpret

The cosine of the angle (and hence the angle itself) depends on the gravitational force per unit mass, g, the angular speed, ω, and the length, l, of the string.

2 Explain why the analysis suggests that the heavier bob will swing out at the same angle as the lighter bob.

Validate

This may be validated by tying two bobs (one heavy and one light) to the spindle of the conical pendulum using strings of the same length. A visual check will show that they both swing out at the same angle.

3 Use the analysis to solve, interpret and (where possible) validate the following problems.

   (a) What happens to the angle θ as the angular speed ω increases?

   (b) How big can the angle become?

   (c) What happens if you keep the angular speed the same but increase the length of the string?

   (d) Explain why h is the same for two bobs of different masses, tied to the spindle with different lengths of string.

Sometimes, a mathematical analysis of a problem suggests 'solutions' to new problems. For example, it is interesting to note that for the conical pendulum:

$$\cos \theta \leqslant 1 \Rightarrow \frac{g}{l\omega^2} \leqslant 1 \Rightarrow \omega \geqslant \sqrt{\left(\frac{g}{l}\right)}$$

4 What happens if $\omega < \sqrt{\left(\frac{g}{l}\right)}$?

What does this tell you about the motion of a conical pendulum?

5 What is the main difference between a chair-o-plane and a conical pendulum?

2 Work and kinetic energy

2.1 Areas under graphs

Measurements taken during a simulation of a car crash produced the graph shown below.

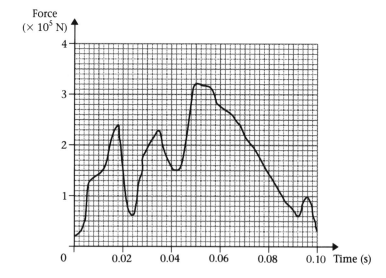

 If the mass of the car was 1200 kg, estimate the original speed of the car if it came to rest after 0.1 second.

 TASKSHEET 1 — The moving car (page 27)

You found that the area under the (time, force) graph represented the change in momentum.

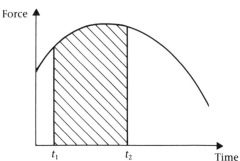

The direction of the force was constant, although the magnitude varied. Newton's second law of motion states:

$$\mathbf{F} = \frac{\mathrm{d}}{\mathrm{d}t}(m\mathbf{v})$$

From the fundamental theorem of calculus it follows that:

$$\int_{t_1}^{t_2} \mathbf{F}\,\mathrm{d}t = m\mathbf{v}_2 - m\mathbf{v}_1$$

where $\mathbf{v}_1$ and $\mathbf{v}_2$ are the velocities at t_1 and t_2 respectively. It therefore follows that the area under any (time, force) graph represents change in momentum. The change in momentum due to a force is known as the **impulse** of the force and is measured in newton seconds (Ns).

> The area under a (time, force) graph represents change in momentum.

E X A M P L E   1

The force acting on a golf ball of mass 45 g when it is struck may be modelled approximately by the function:

$$F = 10^{11}t(t - 0.004)^2 \qquad 0 < t < 0.004$$

Find the velocity with which it leaves the club.

13

SOLUTION

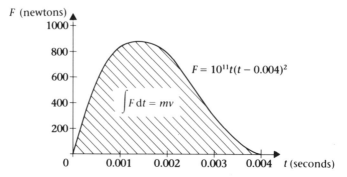

The area under the graph gives the change in momentum, or impulse. Since the initial velocity (and hence momentum) is zero, the momentum of the ball when it leaves the club face is represented by the area:

$$mv = 10^{11} \int_0^{0.004} t(t - 0.004)^2 \, dt$$

$$0.045v = 2.13$$

$$\Rightarrow v = 47 \, \text{m s}^{-1}$$

The integral can be evaluated numerically, using a suitable algorithm on a computer, or algebraically, by multiplying out the bracket.

The ball leaves the club face with an initial velocity of $47 \, \text{m s}^{-1}$ in the direction of the force.

EXERCISE 1

1 A ball of mass 90 grams strikes a wall at right-angles when moving at $8 \, \text{m s}^{-1}$. It rebounds along the same line with a speed of $6 \, \text{m s}^{-1}$. A very simple force–time model assumes that the force between the wall and the ball increases uniformly with time up to a maximum and then decreases at the same rate. Use this model to estimate the maximum force (in newtons) on the ball if the total contact time is 0.002 seconds.

2 A car of mass 1 tonne started from rest and accelerated for 60 seconds. During this time the propulsive force was measured at 10-second intervals.

Force (N)	1050	650	480	260	170	130	80
Time (s)	0	10	20	30	40	50	60

Use this information to estimate the final speed of the car.

3 A ball of mass 0.5 kg is moving with velocity $\begin{bmatrix} 8 \\ 4 \end{bmatrix}$ ms^{-1} when it receives a blow that changes its velocity to $\begin{bmatrix} 4 \\ 6 \end{bmatrix}$ ms^{-1}. What was the impulse due to the blow?

4

When a car runs off the road into a certain type of wire crash-barrier, the force exerted by the barrier on the car is given approximately by the function $F = 42000 \sin(2\pi t)$, where F is measured in newtons and t in seconds. This force acts perpendicular to the barrier.

A car of mass 1200 kg hits such a barrier at an angle of 30° while travelling at 20 ms^{-1}. The impact lasts 0.5 second.

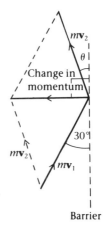

(a) Evaluate the impulse of the force, i.e. $\int_0^{0.5} 42000 \sin(2\pi t)\, dt$.

(b) Explain why the change in momentum is perpendicular to the barrier.

(c) Calculate the initial momentum of the car.

(d) Find the momentum of the car after impact by scale drawing or otherwise.

(e) What is the velocity of the car after impact?

2.2 Speed and distance

Was one of the cars involved in this accident speeding? Police and insurance claim investigators need to know at what speed a vehicle was travelling before the brakes were applied. The length of time taken for skidding cannot be measured but the distance of the skid is often easy to measure.

You are familiar with the momentum equation for motion under a constant force:

$$\mathbf{F}t = m\mathbf{v} - m\mathbf{u}$$

If the force is in the direction of motion, this becomes a relationship between **speed** and **time**:

$$Ft = mv - mu$$

This section investigates the relationship between **speed** and **distance**.

A series of skid tests is carried out in which a car skids to rest with its wheels locked by the brakes. The table below shows the lengths of skid marks, x metres, for various speeds, $u\,\mathrm{km\,h^{-1}}$.

u	0	40	60	80	100
x	0	9	20	36	56

What would you expect the length of the skid marks to be for an initial speed of $120\,\mathrm{km\,h^{-1}}$? Find x in terms of u.

An object of mass m is accelerated in a straight line by a constant force F, from speed u to speed v. Its (t, v) graph is as shown.

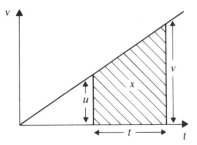

Find the distance covered, x, in terms of u, v and t.

Use the equation $Ft = mv - mu$ to obtain the expression:

$$Fx = \tfrac{1}{2}mv^2 - \tfrac{1}{2}mu^2$$

for the product, force $\times$ distance.

The concept of 'force $\times$ distance' is as useful as that for 'force $\times$ time' which you have used previously. The expenditure of energy involved in pushing something along for some distance has come to be known as 'doing work'. To be more precise, the product Fx is known by engineers, physicists and mathematicians as the **work** done by the force.

The energy of motion acquired by the object as a result of being pushed (and having 'work' done on it) is represented by $\tfrac{1}{2}mv^2$. This form of energy is called **kinetic energy**, from the Greek word for motion, κινησις (kinesis). Other forms of energy will be introduced later in this unit.

For a constant force accelerating an object in a straight line:

$$Fx = \tfrac{1}{2}mv^2 - \tfrac{1}{2}mu^2$$

work done = change in kinetic energy

The units of energy are known as **joules** (abbreviated to J). These are named after James Prescott Joule (1818–89), an English physicist who established that the various forms of energy known at that time – mechanical, electrical and heat – are basically the same. Each can be transformed into any of the others.

1 N m (from force × distance) is the same as 1 joule.
Also, $1 \, \text{kg} \, \text{m}^2 \text{s}^{-2}$ (from $\frac{1}{2}$ mass × speed^2) is the same as 1 joule.

> What is the kinetic energy, in joules, of a 1 kg mass travelling
> with a speed of $1 \, \text{m} \, \text{s}^{-1}$?

EXAMPLE 2

(a) A sports car of mass 1000 kg is travelling at $50 \, \text{m} \, \text{s}^{-1}$. What is the
work done by the frictional forces which bring it to rest?

(b) If it is brought to rest in 50 metres, what is the total retarding
force (assumed to be constant)?

SOLUTION

(a) Work done = change in kinetic energy
$$= \tfrac{1}{2}mv^2 - \tfrac{1}{2}mu^2 = \tfrac{1}{2} \times 1000 \times 0^2 - \tfrac{1}{2} \times 1000 \times 50^2$$
$$= -1\,250\,000 \text{ joules}$$

(b) Let the total retarding force be F newtons.
Work done $= F \times 50 = -1\,250\,000$
$$\Rightarrow \quad F = -25\,000 \text{ newtons}$$

> Why is the force negative?

EXAMPLE 3

A car hits a telegraph pole head-on. There are skid marks of length
27 metres, and it is established from analysis of the impact damage
that the car must have been travelling at $55 \, \text{km} \, \text{h}^{-1}$ on impact. A skid
test shows that, in similar circumstances, from the speed of
$70 \, \text{km} \, \text{h}^{-1}$, the car would have been expected to stop in 25 metres. At
what speed was the car travelling when the brakes were applied?

SOLUTION

Speeds in $\text{km} \, \text{h}^{-1}$ must be converted to speeds in $\text{m} \, \text{s}^{-1}$. In this case:
$$70 \, \text{km} \, \text{h}^{-1} \approx 19.5 \, \text{m} \, \text{s}^{-1} \quad \text{and} \quad 55 \, \text{km} \, \text{h}^{-1} \approx 15.3 \, \text{m} \, \text{s}^{-1}$$

For the skid test: let F be the resultant force on the car.
$$F \times 25 = \tfrac{1}{2}m \times 0^2 - \tfrac{1}{2}m \times 19.5^2 \Rightarrow \frac{F}{m} = -7.6$$

For the pre-collision skid:

$$F \times 27 = \tfrac{1}{2}m \times 15.3^2 - \tfrac{1}{2}mu^2$$
$$\Rightarrow \frac{F}{m} \times 27 = \tfrac{1}{2} \times 15.3^2 - \tfrac{1}{2}u^2$$
$$\Rightarrow -7.6 \times 27 = \tfrac{1}{2} \times 15.3^2 - \tfrac{1}{2}u^2$$
$$\Rightarrow u = 25.4$$

When the brakes were applied, the car was travelling at about $25.4\,\mathrm{m\,s^{-1}}$ or $91\,\mathrm{km\,h^{-1}}$.

EXERCISE 2

1 A car of mass 1500 kg is travelling at 150 km h^{-1}. Considering this motion only, and neglecting any energy associated with rotation of moving parts of the car, how much kinetic energy does the car possess? Give your answer in joules.

If the car's brakes are applied, locking the wheels and causing the car to skid to a halt in 100 metres, what is the average retarding force due to friction between the tyres and the road?

2 A bullet of mass 15 grams passes horizontally through a piece of wood 2 cm thick. If its speed is reduced from 500 m s^{-1} to 300 m s^{-1}, find the average resistive force exerted by the wood.

3 A car of mass 1 tonne accelerates with a constant acceleration from 0 to 108 km h^{-1} in 15 seconds. Find the net forward force on the car. If the engine is then switched off and the car is allowed to come to rest under the action of a resistive force of 500 newtons, find the total distance travelled by the car.

4 A car of mass 800 kg is capable of producing a net force of 3100 newtons in first gear, 2000 newtons in second gear, 1500 newtons in third gear and 1100 newtons in top gear. Find the speed attained if the car is driven from rest for 10 metres in first, 20 metres in second, 30 metres in third and 40 metres in top gear.

5 A van of mass 2250 kg hit a low obstruction which caused it to turn on its side and slide 32 metres before hitting a barrier. Impact tests suggest that it hit the barrier at 50 km h^{-1}. Tests involving towing the remains of the van, on its side, on the same road surface in similar conditions, suggest that the friction forces retarding the sliding van amount to about 2×10^4 newtons. At approximately what speed did the van start to slide on its side?

6 Find the kinetic energy of the Earth due to its motion round the Sun. (You may assume the mass of the Earth to be 6.04×10^{24} kg, the mean radius of its orbit to be 1.5×10^8 km and the length of the year to be 365 days.)

2.3 Work done by a variable force

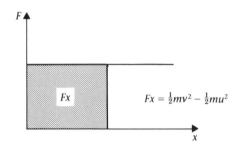

For a constant force **F**, acting in the direction of the displacement x, the area under the (displacement, force) graph is the work done and equals the change in kinetic energy. Considering a (displacement, force) graph will help you to see how to calculate the work done by a variable force.

A car of mass 1 tonne, starting from rest, experiences a net forward force **F** (taking account of resistances to motion). During the first 50 metres of motion, the force is as given in the table below:

Distance travelled (metres), x	5	15	25	35	45
Net forward force (newtons), F	3800	3675	3500	3275	3000

(a) Estimate the speed of the car after it has travelled 10, 20, 30, 40 and 50 metres.

(b) How would you expect the result:

$$Fx = \tfrac{1}{2}mv^2 - \tfrac{1}{2}mu^2$$

to generalise for a variable force? Justify your answer as carefully as possible.

You saw earlier that the area under a (time, force) graph represents the **change in momentum**.

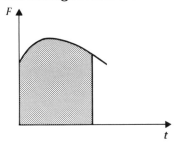

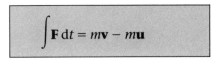

$$\int \mathbf{F}\,dt = m\mathbf{v} - m\mathbf{u}$$

For a constant force this simplifies to:

$$\mathbf{F}t = m\mathbf{v} - m\mathbf{u}$$

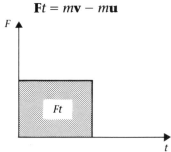

Similarly, for a force in the direction of displacement, the area under a (displacement, force) graph represents **work** and equals the **change in kinetic energy**.

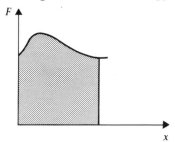

$$\int F\,dx = \tfrac{1}{2}mv^2 - \tfrac{1}{2}mu^2$$

For a constant force, this simplifies to:

$$Fx = \tfrac{1}{2}mv^2 - \tfrac{1}{2}mu^2$$

The change in momentum and the change in kinetic energy equations can both be shown to be integrals of Newton's second law, $\mathbf{F} = m\mathbf{a}$. It is often considerably easier to apply these equations than to use Newton's second law.

21

EXAMPLE 4

A car of mass 1 tonne, starting from rest, experiences a resultant force F newtons. During the first 50 metres of motion, the force is related to the distance travelled, x, by the relationship $F = 4025 - x^2$.

Calculate the speed of the car after it has travelled 50 metres.

SOLUTION

$$\text{Total work done} = \int_0^{50} (4025 - x^2)\, dx$$

$$= \left[4025x - \tfrac{1}{3}x^3 \right]_0^{50} \approx 159\,600\,\text{J}$$

Total work done = change in kinetic energy
$$159\,600 = \tfrac{1}{2} \times 1000 \times v^2 - 0 \Rightarrow 319.2 = v^2$$

The speed is approximately $17.9\,\text{m s}^{-1}$.

EXERCISE 3

1   An object of mass 10 kg is accelerated from rest by a machine with the following force–distance relationship:

Distance (metres)	0	1	2	3	4	5	6	7	8
Force (newtons)	400	300	240	210	190	160	130	80	0

Estimate the speed of the object at intervals of one metre during the thrust.

2   The effective force forward, F newtons, on a van of mass 1.4 tonnes accelerating from rest, is given by the equation $F = 4000 - 22.5x - 0.25x^2$, where x metres is the distance travelled from rest.

Find, by integration, the speed achieved by the van when it has gone 50 metres.

3   A car of mass 1 tonne starts from rest on a level road. The net forward force is initially 3300 newtons but this falls in proportion to the distance travelled so that after 200 metres its value is zero. Find the force in terms of x. Hence find the speed of the car every 50 metres and sketch a graph to show the relationship between the speed and the distance travelled.

4   A stone is dropped down a well and takes 3 seconds to reach the bottom. Find the speed with which the stone hits the bottom. Use the work–energy equation to find the depth of the well. [Take $g = 10\,\text{m s}^{-2}$.]

2.4 Collisions

In earlier work you have seen that momentum is conserved. However, knowledge of this fact alone will not enable you to predict the outcome of collisions, as illustrated by the following three experiments.

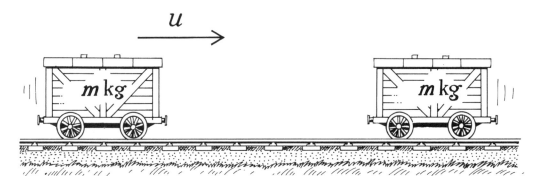

Before collision   **After collision**

$m \xrightarrow{u}$	m	m	$m \xrightarrow{u}$
$m \xrightarrow{u}$	m	$m \xrightarrow{} \frac{u}{2}$	$m \xrightarrow{} \frac{u}{2}$
$m \xrightarrow{u}$	m	$m \xrightarrow{} \frac{u}{4}$	$m \xrightarrow{} \frac{3u}{4}$

(a) Check that momentum is conserved in all three collisions.

(b) The three collisions involve the trucks

   (i) coupling together,   (ii) using spring buffers,
(iii) using cork buffers.

   Which is which?

(c) Is kinetic energy conserved in any or all of these collisions?

Although momentum is always conserved, you have seen that the same is not necessarily true for kinetic energy.

> Kinetic energy is often lost when two bodies collide. A collision in which there is no loss of kinetic energy is called a **perfectly elastic collision**.

If two objects collide along a straight line and if you can assume that both kinetic energy and momentum are conserved, then it is not too difficult to obtain an interesting and very useful result.

Consider the following collision where both kinetic energy and momentum are conserved.

Speed of approach $= u_1 - u_2$ Speed of separation $= v_2 - v_1$

$$\boxed{m_1} \overset{u_1}{\rightarrow} \quad \boxed{m_2} \overset{u_2}{\rightarrow} \qquad\qquad \boxed{m_1} \overset{v_1}{\rightarrow} \quad \boxed{m_2} \overset{v_2}{\rightarrow}$$

Kinetic energy: $\frac{1}{2}m_1u_1^2 + \frac{1}{2}m_2u_2^2 = \frac{1}{2}m_1v_1^2 + \frac{1}{2}m_2v_2^2$

Momentum: $m_1u_1 + m_2u_2 = m_1v_1 + m_2v_2$

$\Rightarrow m_1(u_1^2 - v_1^2) \quad = m_2(v_2^2 - u_2^2) \quad$ and $\quad m_1(u_1 - v_1) = m_2(v_2 - u_2)$

$$\Rightarrow \frac{m_1(u_1^2 - v_1^2)}{m_1(u_1 - v_1)} = \frac{m_2(v_2^2 - u_2^2)}{m_2(v_2 - u_2)}$$

$$\Rightarrow \frac{(u_1 - v_1)(u_1 + v_1)}{(u_1 - v_1)} = \frac{(v_2 - u_2)(v_2 + u_2)}{(v_2 - u_2)}$$

$\Rightarrow u_1 + v_1 = v_2 + u_2$

$\Rightarrow u_1 - u_2 = v_2 - v_1$

This result shows that the speed of separation is the **same** as the speed of approach. Although the analysis above only considers the particular case when the velocities before and after collision are all in the same direction, it is true for all perfectly elastic collisions.

In a perfectly elastic collision, the speed with which the colliding objects separate is the **same** as the speed with which they initially approached each other.

> For a perfectly elastic collision:
>
>   speed of separation = speed of approach

This fact, together with the principle of conservation of momentum, can be used to predict the outcome of perfectly elastic collisions.

EXAMPLE 5

Predict the outcome of this collision $\boxed{3m} \overset{u}{\rightarrow} \qquad \boxed{m}$
between trucks with spring buffers.

SOLUTION

Assume the collision is perfectly elastic so the speed of separation must also be u.

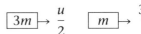

For conservation of momentum,

$$3\not{m}v + \not{m}(v + u) = 3\not{m}u$$
$$\Rightarrow \quad 3v + v + u = 3u$$
$$\Rightarrow \quad 4v = 2u$$
$$\Rightarrow \quad v = \frac{u}{2}$$

giving speeds of $\dfrac{u}{2}$ and $\dfrac{3u}{2}$, as shown.

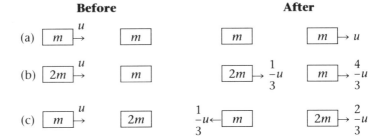

EXERCISE 4

1   Consider the following three perfectly elastic collisions between trucks which each have spring buffers.

Before   **After**

(a) $m \xrightarrow{u}$ m m $m \rightarrow u$

(b) $2m \xrightarrow{u}$ m $2m \rightarrow \frac{1}{3}u$ $m \rightarrow \frac{4}{3}u$

(c) $m \xrightarrow{u}$ $2m$ $\frac{1}{3}u \leftarrow m$ $2m \rightarrow \frac{2}{3}u$

For each of the collisions above, show that:

(i) momentum is conserved;   (ii) kinetic energy is conserved;

(iii) speed of separation = speed of approach.

2   (a) Two trucks, each of mass m, approach each other from opposite directions, each travelling with speed v. Assuming the collision to be perfectly elastic, what will be the speed of each truck after the collision?

(b) If the experiment is repeated with one of the trucks now having speed $2v$, what will be the velocity of each truck after the collision?

(c) Compare the total kinetic energy of the two trucks before and after each collision.

   TASKSHEET 2E – Sporting collisions (page 28)

After working through this chapter you should:

1 know that for one-dimensional motion, the area under a
   (time, force) graph represents the change in momentum or
   impulse:

$$\int \mathbf{F} \, dt = m\mathbf{v} - m\mathbf{u}$$

2 know that for one-dimensional motion the area under a
   (displacement, force) graph represents work done and equals the
   change in kinetic energy and:

$$\int F \, dx = \tfrac{1}{2}mv^2 - \tfrac{1}{2}mu^2$$

3 know that momentum is conserved in all collisions, but that
   kinetic energy is conserved only in a perfectly elastic collision;

4 know that in a perfectly elastic collision, the speed of separation
   is equal to the speed of approach.

The moving car

Consider a car accelerating in a straight line along a horizontal stretch of road. The forces acting on the car in motion are:

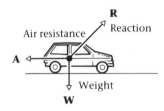

$$F = A + W + R$$

The car has mass 800 kg and accelerates from 0 to $30\,\mathrm{m\,s^{-1}}$ in 20 seconds. The velocity of the car is modelled by the functions:

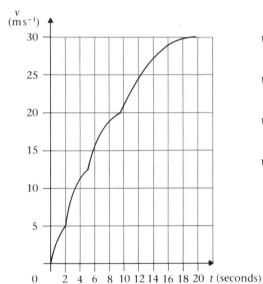

$$v = \frac{-5t^2 + 20t}{4} \qquad 0 < t \leqslant 2$$

$$v = \frac{-7t^2 + 70t - 67}{9} \qquad 2 < t \leqslant 5$$

$$v = \frac{-8t^2 + 160t - 300}{25} \qquad 5 < t \leqslant 10$$

$$v = \frac{-t^2 + 40t - 100}{10} \qquad 10 < t \leqslant 20$$

1   At the times $t = 1, 3$ and 7 seconds,

   (a) evaluate the momentum of the car;

   (b) find the acceleration of the car;

   (c) find the resultant force acting on the car.

2   (a) Sketch the (time, momentum) graph for $0 < t < 10$.

   (b) Sketch the (time, force) graph for $0 < t < 10$.

3   Evaluate the area under the (time, force) graph. What does this area represent?

Sporting collisions

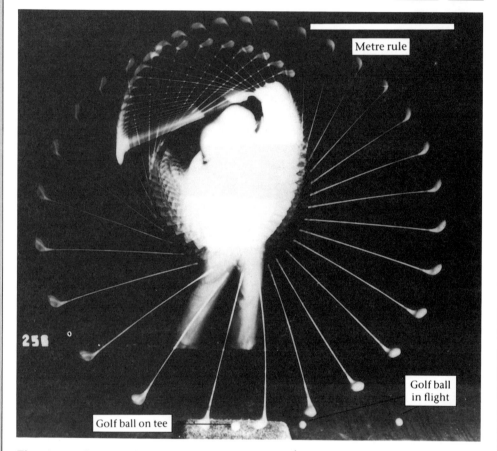

Metre rule

25 B

Golf ball in flight

Golf ball on tee

The picture shows strobe photographs, taken every $\frac{1}{100}$th of a second, of a golfer striking a golf ball.

1   Use measurements taken from the photograph to find the speed of the head of the golf club just before the collision and the speed of the golf ball after being struck.

The speed of the golf ball is less than twice the initial speed of the club. This initial speed of the club is determined by the golfer's technique and physique. It is important to know how this limits the speed of the golf ball.

You can model the striking of the golf ball by an elastic collision of a mass M with a stationary mass m.

$$ (M) \xrightarrow{u} (m) $$

2   Comment upon whether these assumptions are reasonable. What, in your opinion, is the most significant difference between this mathematical model and reality?

After the collision the speeds are:

$\textcircled{M} \overset{v-u}{\rightarrow} \quad \textcircled{m} \overset{v}{\rightarrow}$

where:

$$M(v - u) + mv = Mu$$
$$\Rightarrow \quad (M + m)v = 2Mu$$
$$\Rightarrow \quad \frac{v}{u} = \frac{2M}{M + m}$$

and so $\dfrac{v}{u}$ can never be greater than 2.

3 (a) Explain why the speeds after the collision can be taken to be v and $v - u$.

(b) Justify the equation $M(v - u) + mv = Mu$.

(c) Explain why $\dfrac{2M}{M + m}$ can never be greater than 2.

When a mass with speed u collides with a smaller stationary mass, the resulting speed of the small mass is limited to $2u$. This value is achieved approximately in golf and whenever the stationary mass is relatively very small.

As you have seen, golf is a sporting example of $\dfrac{v}{u}$ being maximised. You can also investigate what relative values of the masses will maximise the proportion of the initial kinetic energy which is transferred to the second object.

The initial kinetic energy is $\frac{1}{2}Mu^2$ and so the proportion transferred is:

$$\frac{\frac{1}{2}mv^2}{\frac{1}{2}Mu^2} = \frac{m}{M}\left(\frac{v}{u}\right)^2$$

$$= \frac{m}{M}\left(2\frac{M}{M+m}\right)^2 = \frac{4\dfrac{m}{M}}{\left(1 + \dfrac{m}{M}\right)^2}$$

4 Show that the maximum value, for positive x, of the function $\dfrac{4x}{(1 + x)^2}$ is 1.

Find the value of x for which this maximum occurs.

The maximum proportion of kinetic energy transferred is therefore 1. This occurs when $x = 1$, i.e. when $m = M$.

5 Describe a sporting example of this situation.

3 Using scalar products

3.1 Work done in two dimensions

A lifebelt is thrown horizontally from a ship and lands in the water near a swimmer.

If its initial velocity is $\begin{bmatrix} u \\ 0 \end{bmatrix}$ explain why:

(a) $\mathbf{v} = \begin{bmatrix} u \\ -gt \end{bmatrix}$ (b) $\mathbf{r} = \begin{bmatrix} ut \\ -\frac{1}{2}gt^2 \end{bmatrix}$

The deck of the ship is 20 metres above sea level and the lifebelt has mass 3 kg. Assume $g = 10\,\mathrm{N\,kg^{-1}}$.

Suppose the lifebelt is projected horizontally with speed:

(a) $10\,\mathrm{m\,s^{-1}}$ (b) $20\,\mathrm{m\,s^{-1}}$ (c) $30\,\mathrm{m\,s^{-1}}$ (d) $u\,\mathrm{m\,s^{-1}}$

For each speed of projection calculate:

  (i) the displacement vector, **r**, of the swimmer from the deck;

 (ii) the change in the kinetic energy of the lifebelt from the point of projection to when it lands in the water.

What does this suggest about work done on the belt during this time?

Calculate the work done by gravity if the lifebelt is **dropped** from the deck into the sea.

You have seen that, in one dimension, the work done by the resultant force acting on a body is equal to the change in kinetic energy of the body. For projectile motion, if you ignore air resistance, gravity is the only force acting. The work done by gravity is independent of the horizontal displacement of the body and is equal to the change in kinetic energy. When several forces act on a body, each force may do work. However, the change in kinetic energy is caused by the work done by the resultant force. In the situation above, only one force is assumed to be acting, so the work done by gravity is equal to the change in kinetic energy.

In addition, in one-dimensional situations, work done was defined as force × distance.

Work done $= F \times d$

In the example of the lifebelt, even though the direction of the motion was not the same as the direction of the force acting, work was done by gravity to change the kinetic energy of the belt. You saw that:

    work done = magnitude of weight × vertical distance travelled

In general, the work done by a constant force is defined as the product of the magnitude of the force and the distance moved in the direction of the force.

The work done is $F \times d$
$$= Fr\cos\theta$$

31

EXAMPLE 1

A child of mass 30 kg is sliding down a slide of length 4 metres inclined at 40° to the vertical. What work does the gravitational force do?

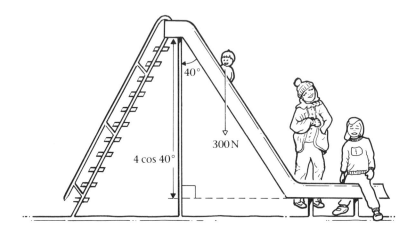

SOLUTION

Work done $= Fr \cos \theta$
$$= 300 \times 4 \cos 40°$$
$$= 919 \text{ joules}$$

EXERCISE 1

1   A ski-jumper of mass 75 kg is practising on a dry ski slope. He travels 35 metres down a slope inclined at 55° to the vertical. What is the work done by gravity?

2   A trolley of mass 15 kg is pulled up a ramp, inclined at 25° to the horizontal, by means of a rope parallel to the slope. If the tension in the rope is 100 newtons, find the work done by this force when the trolley is raised 5 metres vertically.

3   A sledge of mass 10 kg slides 25 metres down a slope. If the work done by gravity is 500 joules, what is the angle of elevation of the slope?

4   A girl of mass 50 kg walks 100 metres up a slope of 30° to the horizontal. What is the work done against gravity?

3.2 The scalar product

The work done by a constant force **F** displaced through a vector **r** is written as **F** . **r**, (read as **F** 'dot' **r**) and is called the **scalar product** of vectors **F** and **r**. (It is called a product because it involves multiplication and it is called a scalar because the result is **not** a vector.)

E X A M P L E   2

Calculate the scalar product **F** . **r** in the following instances.

(a)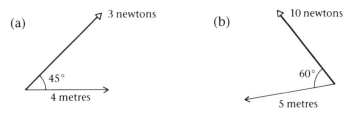

(b)

S O L U T I O N

(a) **F** . **r** = $3 \times 4 \times \cos 45° = 8.5$ joules

(b) **F** . **r** = $10 \times 5 \times \cos 60° = 25$ joules

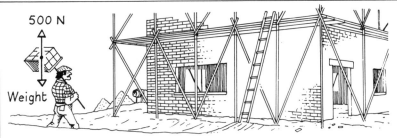

A labourer has to move bricks from the ground floor to the first floor of a building. Using a hod to carry the bricks, he walks up a 4 metre slope of angle 15° and then climbs a 5 metre ladder inclined at 70° attached to the scaffolding. The force he exerts on the bricks is modelled as a constant vertical force of magnitude 500 newtons.

What is the work done by the 500 newton force acting on the bricks?

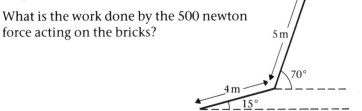

The work done by a constant force **F** when displaced through a vector **r** is:

$$\mathbf{F} . \mathbf{r} = Fr \cos \theta$$

where θ is the angle between the directions of **F** and **r**.

 TASKSHEET 1 — Investigating the scalar product (page 47)

Suppose that a force **F** is displaced through a vector **r**.

- When $\theta = 0°$ the work done is *Fr*.

  If the force and displacement are in the same direction then the work done is simply force times distance.

- When $\theta = 90°$ the work done is zero.

  If the direction of the force and displacement are at right angles to each other, then the distance moved in the direction of the force is zero and no work is done.

- $(k\mathbf{F}) . \mathbf{r} = kFr \cos \theta$
  $\qquad\qquad = Fkr \cos \theta$
  $\qquad\qquad = \mathbf{F} . k\mathbf{r}$

  If the magnitude of either the force or the displacement is increased by a factor of k, then the work done is also increased by a factor of k.

- $\mathbf{F} . (\mathbf{r} + \mathbf{s}) = \mathbf{F} . \mathbf{r} + \mathbf{F} . \mathbf{s}$

  work done from A to C = $\mathbf{F} . (\mathbf{r} + \mathbf{s})$
  work done from A to B = $\mathbf{F} . \mathbf{r}$
  work done from B to C = $\mathbf{F} . \mathbf{s}$

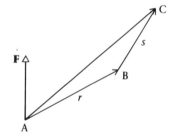

- $\mathbf{F} . \mathbf{r} = F \times r \cos \theta$
  $\qquad\quad = r \times F \cos \theta$
  $\qquad\quad = \mathbf{r} . \mathbf{F}$

  Work done is also the component of the force in the direction moved multiplied by the distance moved.

34

EXAMPLE 3

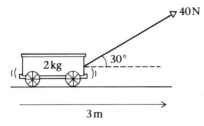

A trolley of mass 2 kg is pulled along the floor by a string held at an angle of 30° to the horizontal.

If the tension in the string is 40 newtons, find the work done by this force in pulling the trolley 3 metres across the floor.

SOLUTION

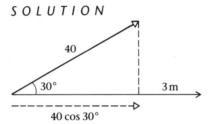

Work done $= \mathbf{r} \cdot \mathbf{F}$
$= rF \cos \theta$
$= 3 \times 40 \cos 30°$
$= 103.9 \text{J}$

EXERCISE 2

1 A force of 5 newtons acts on a particle at A, which is displaced 4 metres along AB. (a) Calculate the work done by the force.

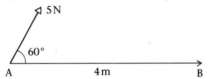

(b) If the direction of the force is reversed but the displacement remains the same, i.e. $\overrightarrow{AB}$, calculate the work done by this new force.

2 Calculate the scalar product of the following pairs of vectors.

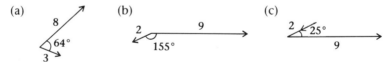

3 A roller is pulled 7 metres across a cricket pitch. The handle is pulled with a force of 100 newtons at an angle of 40° to the vertical.

(a) What is the work done by this force?

(b) What is the work done if the handle is pushed with the same force?

4 A horse pulls a barge of mass 30 tonnes along a canal by means of a rope which makes an angle of 20° with the direction of the barge.

If the tension in the rope is 200 newtons, find the work done by this force in pulling the barge 1 km.

3.3 Using column vectors

What is the work done when a force $\mathbf{F} = \begin{bmatrix} 3 \\ 3 \end{bmatrix}$ newtons moves

its point of application through a displacement $\mathbf{r} = \begin{bmatrix} 0 \\ 4 \end{bmatrix}$ metres?

A force $\mathbf{F} = \begin{bmatrix} a \\ b \end{bmatrix}$ can be replaced

by forces $\mathbf{a} = \begin{bmatrix} a \\ 0 \end{bmatrix}$ and $\mathbf{b} = \begin{bmatrix} 0 \\ b \end{bmatrix}$

Similarly, a displacement $\mathbf{r} = \begin{bmatrix} c \\ d \end{bmatrix}$ can be written as $\mathbf{r} = \mathbf{c} + \mathbf{d}$

where $\mathbf{c} = \begin{bmatrix} c \\ 0 \end{bmatrix}$ and $\mathbf{d} = \begin{bmatrix} 0 \\ d \end{bmatrix}$

So $\mathbf{F} \cdot \mathbf{r} = (\mathbf{a} + \mathbf{b}) \cdot (\mathbf{c} + \mathbf{d})$
$= \mathbf{a} \cdot \mathbf{c} + \mathbf{a} \cdot \mathbf{d} + \mathbf{b} \cdot \mathbf{c} + \mathbf{b} \cdot \mathbf{d}$
$= ac \cos 0° + ad \cos 90° + bc \cos 90° + bd \cos 0°$
$= ac + bd$

(a) Use this result to check the answer to the question posed in the thinking point above.

(b) What are the advantages/disadvantages of this method for calculating the work done by a force?

When a force $\mathbf{F} = \begin{bmatrix} a \\ b \end{bmatrix}$ moves its point of application a

distance $\mathbf{r} = \begin{bmatrix} x \\ y \end{bmatrix}$ then the work done by the force is:

$$\mathbf{F} \cdot \mathbf{r} = \begin{bmatrix} a \\ b \end{bmatrix} \cdot \begin{bmatrix} x \\ y \end{bmatrix} = ax + by$$

i.e., the value of the work done is obtained by first multiplying the corresponding elements together and then summing the results.

EXAMPLE 4

A particle is acted upon by two forces $\begin{bmatrix} 3 \\ 4 \end{bmatrix}$ and $\begin{bmatrix} 5 \\ -12 \end{bmatrix}$ newtons.

If it is displaced through $\begin{bmatrix} 16 \\ -16 \end{bmatrix}$ metres, find the work done by each of the forces.

SOLUTION

Work done by the $\begin{bmatrix} 3 \\ 4 \end{bmatrix}$ force is $\begin{bmatrix} 3 \\ 4 \end{bmatrix} \cdot \begin{bmatrix} 16 \\ -16 \end{bmatrix} = 48 + -64 = -16$ joules

Work done by the $\begin{bmatrix} 5 \\ -12 \end{bmatrix}$ force is $\begin{bmatrix} 5 \\ -12 \end{bmatrix} \cdot \begin{bmatrix} 16 \\ -16 \end{bmatrix} = 80 + 192 = 272$ joules

EXERCISE 3

1 Find the work done when a force **F** newtons acts on a particle which subsequently moves through a displacement **r** metres where:

(a) $\mathbf{F} = \begin{bmatrix} 2 \\ 4 \end{bmatrix}$, $\mathbf{r} = \begin{bmatrix} 12 \\ -4 \end{bmatrix}$ (b) $\mathbf{F} = \begin{bmatrix} 1 \\ -2 \end{bmatrix}$, $\mathbf{r} = \begin{bmatrix} -3 \\ 4 \end{bmatrix}$

2 A force of $\begin{bmatrix} 3 \\ -5 \end{bmatrix}$ newtons acts on a particle moving parallel to the vector $\begin{bmatrix} 5 \\ 12 \end{bmatrix}$.

If the work done by the force is 90 joules what is the distance travelled?

3 Forces of $\begin{bmatrix} 3 \\ -3 \end{bmatrix}$ and $\begin{bmatrix} 9 \\ 15 \end{bmatrix}$ newtons act on a particle. If its displacement is parallel to the resultant of the two forces and the total work done by both forces is 120 joules, find the displacement.

4 A particle of mass 5 kg is moved 12 metres down a slope inclined at an angle θ to the horizontal where $\tan \theta = 0.75$. Find the work done by:

(a) the gravitational force, (b) the normal contact force.

5 The work done by a force **F** displaced through vector **r** is $Fr \cos \theta$.

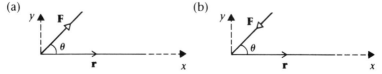

Does the definition $\mathbf{F} \cdot \mathbf{r} = Fr \cos \theta$ hold for both of these diagrams?

3.4 **Work done by several forces**

A stationary engine pulls a load at a constant speed up a slope with gradient 1 in 4. The load is pulled along a channel which has been smoothed by the constant passage of material, so that the frictional force opposing the motion of the load is negligible. The load is pulled from A to B.

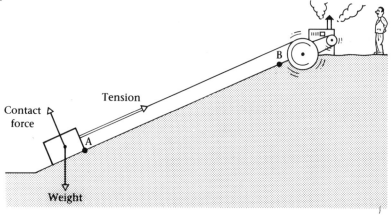

The forces acting on the load are shown below in column vector form. The forces are measured in newtons and the displacement in metres.

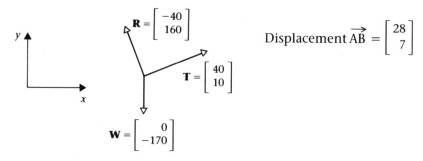

$$\mathbf{R} = \begin{bmatrix} -40 \\ 160 \end{bmatrix}$$

$$\text{Displacement } \overrightarrow{AB} = \begin{bmatrix} 28 \\ 7 \end{bmatrix}$$

$$\mathbf{T} = \begin{bmatrix} 40 \\ 10 \end{bmatrix}$$

$$\mathbf{W} = \begin{bmatrix} 0 \\ -170 \end{bmatrix}$$

In the example above:

(a) calculate the work done by each of the three forces.

(b) What is the resultant force acting on the load?

(c) What work is done by the resultant force?

(d) What is the total work done on the load?

(e) Explain what you have found.

TASKSHEET 2 – Work done by several forces (page 49)

Several of the forces acting on an object may do work on the object, but it is the **total** work done by all the forces on the object which accounts for its final change in kinetic energy.

> The energy equation
>
> > work done = change in kinetic energy
>
> refers to the work done on an object by the **resultant force**.

This result follows directly from the **distributive law**.

Consider two forces **S** and **T** acting on an object. If the displacement of the object is **r**, then:

$$\mathbf{S} \cdot \mathbf{r} + \mathbf{T} \cdot \mathbf{r} = (\mathbf{S} + \mathbf{T}) \cdot \mathbf{r}$$

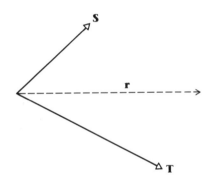

The sum of the work done by each of the two forces equals the work done by the resultant of the two forces.

It is often necessary to calculate the change in kinetic energy of an object when solving certain types of problem.

When calculating the change in kinetic energy you can either:

(a) calculate the work done by the resultant force,

or:

(b) calculate the sum of the work done by the individual forces.

In complicated examples the second method is often preferred, especially if you can identify one of the forces as 'doing no work'.

EXAMPLE 5

A swimmer of weight 700 newtons slides into a swimming pool down a 5 metre long straight chute inclined at 30° to the horizontal. (Assume a constant friction force of 100 newtons.)

(a) Draw a diagram showing the forces acting on the swimmer.

(b) With what speed does the swimmer enter the water?

SOLUTION

(a)

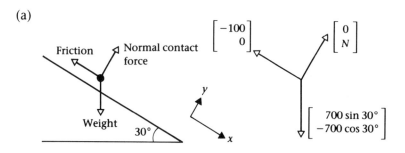

(b) The displacement is $\begin{bmatrix} 5 \\ 0 \end{bmatrix}$.

To calculate the speed of the swimmer you must calculate the total work done and hence the change in kinetic energy (KE).

$$\text{Work done} = \begin{bmatrix} 700 \sin 30° \\ -700 \cos 30° \end{bmatrix} \cdot \begin{bmatrix} 5 \\ 0 \end{bmatrix} + \begin{bmatrix} -100 \\ 0 \end{bmatrix} \cdot \begin{bmatrix} 5 \\ 0 \end{bmatrix} + \begin{bmatrix} 0 \\ N \end{bmatrix} \cdot \begin{bmatrix} 5 \\ 0 \end{bmatrix}$$

$= 1750 - 500 + 0$ joules

Total work done $= 1250$ joules

So change in KE $= 1250$

But change in KE $= \frac{1}{2}mv^2 - \frac{1}{2}mu^2$ where $u = 0$ and $m = 70$

$$\text{so } v^2 = \frac{2 \times 1250}{70}$$

$$v = 6\,\text{m s}^{-1}$$

EXERCISE 4

When answering the following questions state clearly what simplifying
assumptions you make.

1   A ski slope consists of three parts,
    as shown in the diagram. A skier,
    mass 80 kg, starts from rest at A.

    (a) What work is done at each stage?

    (b) What work is done altogether?

    (c) What is the skier's speed at D?

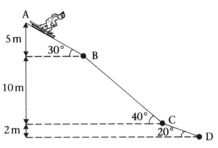

2   A man cycles 50 metres up a slope. The diagram shows a simplified model of
    the forces acting on the cyclist.

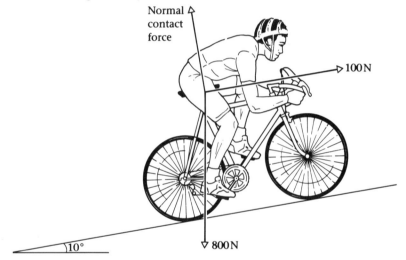

    (a) Suggest what causes the 100 newton force up the slope.

    (b) Calculate the work done by each of the forces shown in the diagram.

    (c) What can you say about the speed with which the man cycles?

3   A girl of weight 450 newtons pulls her small brother, of weight
    300 newtons, on a sledge of weight 40 newtons. She pulls him 80 metres
    along flat ground in a straight line, at a steady speed of $1.2 \, \text{m s}^{-1}$, using a
    rope at $55°$ to the horizontal. Assume the retarding force (friction) is a
    constant 50 newtons.

    (a) Draw a diagram showing the forces acting on the boy.

    (b) What is the work done by each of the forces?

4   A toboggan of mass 5 kg slides from rest down a slope inclined at an angle of
    $\sin^{-1}(\frac{1}{6})$ to the horizontal. After travelling 80 metres it has reached a speed
    of $10 \, \text{m s}^{-1}$. Find the resistance (assumed to be constant).

41

5 A particle of mass 10 grams is initially moving with velocity $\begin{bmatrix} 4 \\ 16 \end{bmatrix}\mathrm{m\,s^{-1}}$.

Later, its velocity is $\begin{bmatrix} 8 \\ -20 \end{bmatrix}\mathrm{m\,s^{-1}}$.

Calculate the work that has been done on the particle.

6 A boy lets go of his sports-bag at the top of a grassy slope inclined at 30° to the horizontal. The bag weighs 10 newtons and is released from rest. If it travels 5 metres down the slope against friction and reaches a speed of $4\,\mathrm{m\,s^{-1}}$, show that the force of friction has magnitude 3.4 newtons. (Use g $= 10\,\mathrm{m\,s^{-2}}$.)

7E A block of mass 6.5 kg is projected with a velocity of $4\,\mathrm{m\,s^{-1}}$ up a line of greatest slope of a rough plane. Calculate the initial kinetic energy of the block.

The coefficient of friction between the block and the plane is $\frac{2}{3}$ and the plane makes an angle θ with the horizontal, where sin $\theta = \frac{5}{13}$. The block travels a distance of d metres up the plane before coming to rest instantaneously. Express in terms of d:

(a) the work done by gravity;

(b) the work done against friction by the block in coming to rest.

Hence calculate the value of d. (Take g as $10\,\mathrm{m\,s^{-2}}$.)

8E A body of mass m is projected up a rough inclined plane with speed $u\,\mathrm{m\,s^{-1}}$ from a point P. It moves up to Q, a distance d from P and then slides back down to P. Show that:

(a) the total work done against friction is $2\,\mu mgd$ cos θ (where μ is the coefficient of friction and θ is the inclination of the plane to the horizontal);

(b) $u = \sqrt{(2gd(\sin \theta + \mu \cos \theta))}$;

(c) the speed of the body when it returns to P is

$$\sqrt{(2gd(\sin \theta - \mu \cos \theta))}$$

3.5 Variable forces

Not all forces acting on an object do work. What can you say about forces which do no work?

(a) What are the forces acting on the bob (mass m) of a pendulum?

(b) Are these forces constant?

(c) What work does each force do when the pendulum moves from A to B?

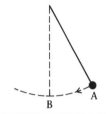

EXAMPLE 6

A circus performer (mass 70 kg) swings on a rope of length 8 metres. He starts from rest, holding the rope at A, 1 metre below the point of suspension. The rope is taut throughout. What is his maximum speed?

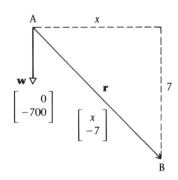

The tension in the rope is a variable force. However, the tension is always perpendicular to the direction of the velocity. Tension therefore does no work.

If air resistance is ignored, the only other force acting on the man is gravity and so it is this force which does the work which changes his kinetic energy.

SOLUTION

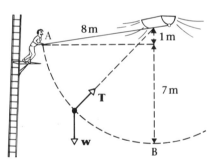

Assume $g = 10 \,\text{N} \text{kg}^{-1} \Rightarrow \mathbf{w} = \begin{bmatrix} 0 \\ -700 \end{bmatrix}$

then $\mathbf{w} \cdot \mathbf{r} = \dfrac{mv^2}{2} - \dfrac{mu^2}{2}$

$\Rightarrow \begin{bmatrix} 0 \\ -700 \end{bmatrix} \cdot \begin{bmatrix} x \\ -7 \end{bmatrix} = \dfrac{70v^2}{2}$ as $u = 0$

$\Rightarrow \quad 4900 = 35v^2$

$\Rightarrow \quad\quad v = 11.8 \,\text{m} \text{s}^{-1}$

How can you be sure the maximum speed is reached at point B?

Would taking the more accurate value g = 9.81 N kg^{-1} make a big difference to your answer?

The man's partner (of smaller mass) performs the same manoeuvre. Will her maximum speed be less than the man's?

A constant force does no work if the direction of its line of action is perpendicular to the displacement of its point of application.

An example is the normal contact force on a straight slide.

A force with variable direction does no work if the object on which it acts has a variable velocity which changes direction in such a way that the direction of the line of application of the force is always perpendicular to the velocity of the object.

An example is the normal contact force on a curved slide.

EXERCISE 5

1   A girl (mass 40 kg) swings on the end of a 5 metre rope in a gymnasium. If she initially jumped at 3 m s^{-1} off a horse 2 metres high on a level 4 metres below the point of suspension of the rope, which was taut, find:

(a) her maximum speed;

(b) her maximum height above
      the ground.

(c) Did you need to know her mass?

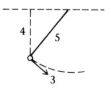

2 A scout sets up an aerial runway starting from 10 metres up a tree.

(a) If the lowest point is 2 metres off the ground, at what speed will someone using the runway pass that point? (State clearly what assumptions you make.)

(b) If the end of the aerial runway is 4 metres off the ground, with what speed will someone reach this point?

(c) Do you think such a runway would be safe?

3 A force of $\begin{bmatrix} 2 \\ 5 \end{bmatrix}$ newtons moves a bead of mass 0.1 kg along a smooth wire from A (6, 7) to B (9, 8).

(a) Calculate the work done by the force.

(b) If the bead starts from rest what is its speed at B?

4 The resultant force on a ball of mass 0.2 kg is $\begin{bmatrix} 6 \\ 5 \end{bmatrix}$ newtons. It causes the ball to move from A $\begin{bmatrix} 6 \\ 7 \end{bmatrix}$ to B $\begin{bmatrix} 10 \\ 12 \end{bmatrix}$.

(a) Calculate the work done by the force.

(b) What can you say about the velocity of the ball at A?

After working through this chapter you should:

1 know that the work done by a constant force **F** is the scalar product **F** . **r** where **r** is the displacement;

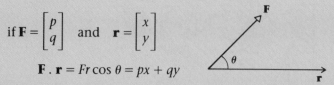

$$\text{if } \mathbf{F} = \begin{bmatrix} p \\ q \end{bmatrix} \quad \text{and} \quad \mathbf{r} = \begin{bmatrix} x \\ y \end{bmatrix}$$

$$\mathbf{F} . \mathbf{r} = Fr \cos \theta = px + qy$$

2 know that the work done by a force may be calculated as either:

   (i) the magnitude of the force multiplied by the distance moved in the direction of the force,

or

   (ii) the magnitude of the displacement multiplied by the component of the force acting in the direction of the displacement;

3 know that the sum of the work done by several forces equals the work done by the resultant force;

4 know that:

change in KE = total work done by all the forces

Investigating the scalar product

1   A man pulls a 20 kg block along a smooth horizontal surface. He exerts a tension of 200 newtons in the chain. Find the work done by the tension in moving the block 4 metres along the surface when the chain makes an angle with the surface of:

(a) 0°   (b) 30°   (c) 60°   (d) 90°

2   Judith calculates the scalar product of the two vectors shown as:

$$5 \times 7 \times \cos 60°$$

Her friend Carole says the angle between the vectors is 300° and therefore calculates the scalar product as:

$$5 \times 7 \times \cos 300°$$

Who is right?

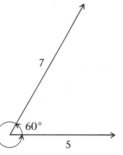

3   A 3.5 kg mass is pulled up a slope inclined at 30° to the horizontal.

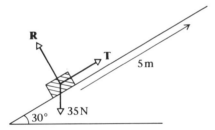

(a) What is the work done by the normal contact force when the mass moves 5 metres up the slope?

(b) What is the work done by the weight in moving 5 metres up the slope?

4   A box is pulled 2 metres across the floor with a force of 30 newtons.

(a) What is the work done by the force?

The box is then pushed back to its original position by a force of 30 newtons.

(b) What is the work done by this force?

(c) What can you say about the size and direction of these forces and displacements?

(d) Explain why $(-\mathbf{p}) \cdot (-\mathbf{q}) = \mathbf{p} \cdot \mathbf{q}$ for any vectors $\mathbf{p}$ and $\mathbf{q}$.

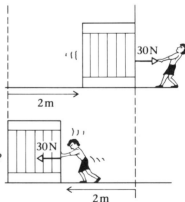

5 (a) A vertical force of 7 newtons lifts a box 7 metres vertically. What is the work done by this force?

 (b) What is $\mathbf{p} \cdot \mathbf{p}$ if $\mathbf{p}$ is any vector?

6 It is estimated that a vertical force of 500 newtons is needed to lift bricks 5 metres up a ramp inclined at 25° to the horizontal.

 (a) What would be the work done by the force?

 (b) How much more work would be done if the bricks had to be moved three times as far up the ramp?

 (c) What would happen to your calculation of work done in part (a) if the force needed to lift the bricks was found to be twice as much as originally estimated?

 (d) How much more work would be done if the force were doubled **and** the distance was three times as far?

 (e) Show that $(k\mathbf{p}) \cdot (l\mathbf{q}) = kl(\mathbf{p} \cdot \mathbf{q})$ for any vectors $\mathbf{p}$ and $\mathbf{q}$ and scalars l and k.

7 A suitcase of mass 10 kg slides 4 metres down a smooth ramp inclined at 25° to the horizontal and then 6 metres down another smooth ramp inclined at 10° to the horizontal. What is the total work done by the weight of the suitcase?

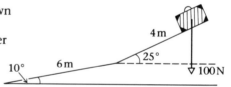

8 The two ramps in question 7 are replaced by a single ramp and an identical suitcase slides down it.

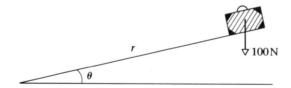

 (a) Find r and θ.

 (b) Find the work done by the weight of the suitcase.

 (c) The identity $\mathbf{p} \cdot (\mathbf{q} + \mathbf{r}) = \mathbf{p} \cdot \mathbf{q} + \mathbf{p} \cdot \mathbf{r}$ is valid for any three vectors $\mathbf{p}$, $\mathbf{q}$ and $\mathbf{r}$. Explain how your answers to the questions above support this statement.

9 A builder can lift bricks with a vertical force of 500 newtons, either up a ramp 5 metres long inclined at 30° to the horizontal, or up another ramp 4 metres long inclined at 48.6° to the horizontal. What would be the difference in the work done by the force?

Work done by several forces

1 Three forces of $\begin{bmatrix} 2 \\ 3 \end{bmatrix}$, $\begin{bmatrix} 4 \\ -1 \end{bmatrix}$ and $\begin{bmatrix} -3 \\ -2 \end{bmatrix}$ newtons act on a particle which is displaced

$\begin{bmatrix} 5 \\ 7 \end{bmatrix}$ metres.

(a) Calculate the work done by each of these forces.

(b) What is the resultant of the three forces?

(c) Calculate the work done by the resultant force.

(d) What is the connection between your answers to (a) and (c)?

2 Repeat question 1 for any three (or more) forces and a displacement of your own choice.

3 Four forces of $\begin{bmatrix} 3 \\ 2 \end{bmatrix}$, $\begin{bmatrix} 4 \\ -8 \end{bmatrix}$, $\begin{bmatrix} 2 \\ -6 \end{bmatrix}$ and $\begin{bmatrix} 3 \\ 6 \end{bmatrix}$ newtons act on an object which

is displaced $\begin{bmatrix} 6 \\ -3 \end{bmatrix}$ metres.

(a) Find the work done by each force.

(b) Find the work done by the resultant of the four forces.

(c) One of the forces does no work. What can you say about its direction?

4 Two forces of $\begin{bmatrix} 22 \\ -4 \end{bmatrix}$ and $\begin{bmatrix} -6 \\ -8 \end{bmatrix}$ newtons act on an object.

Calculate the work done if the object moves 30 cm in the direction $\begin{bmatrix} 4 \\ -3 \end{bmatrix}$.

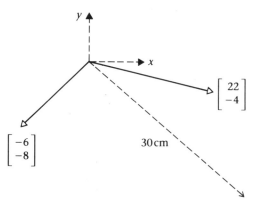

 **Potential energy**

4.1 Gravitational potential energy

Push a pencil across the table in a straight line, keeping its speed constant.

Look at the forces involved in this apparently simple action.

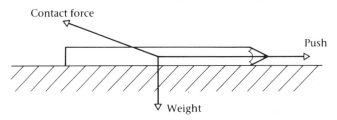

Although only three forces are involved it is sometimes useful to split the contact force into two components, one normal to the table and one parallel to the table.

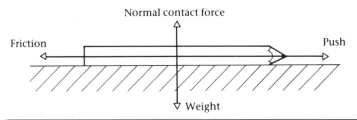

The pencil was stationary before you started to push and it is stationary when you stop pushing, so there is no change in kinetic energy. Does this mean that no work has been done?

Lift a pencil vertically through a height h.

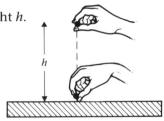

(a) What is the total work done?

(b) What forces act on the pencil?

(c) What is the work done by each force?

You may think that this situation is similar to that of pushing the pencil across the table, but there is one very important difference. When you release the pencil after pushing it across the table, it remains stationary because the friction force vanishes when you stop pushing. When you release the pencil above the table it does not remain stationary. It falls down because gravity is still acting on it. The pencil held at rest above the table has zero kinetic energy, but it can acquire kinetic energy because gravity has the potential to do positive work on it as it falls to the table. For this reason, the pencil is said to have **gravitational potential energy** (PE) before it falls.

If the pencil has mass m kg and the gravitational force per unit mass is g N kg^{-1}, how much kinetic energy could the pencil acquire if it were dropped through a height of h metres?

1   The gravitational potential energy (PE) of a body is always measured relative to an arbitrary fixed reference position where its value is taken to be zero. It is defined as the work that would be done by gravity if the body were to move from its present position to the fixed reference position.

2   A particle of mass m kg, at height h metres above the floor, has gravitational potential energy mgh N m (or joules) relative to the floor.

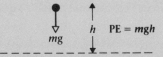

3   If you raise a mass m kg a distance h metres in a vertical direction, you increase the gravitational potential energy by mgh N m, where g is the gravitational force per unit mass.

EXAMPLE 1

Calculate the gravitational potential energy, relative to the ground, of a 2 kg mass at a height of 3 metres above the ground.

SOLUTION

PE = mgh = 2 × 10 × 3
        = 60 joules

Note that the mass has this potential energy whether or not it is allowed to fall.

EXAMPLE 2

A child of mass 20 kg is sitting at the
top of a slide of length 4 metres which
is inclined at 25° to the horizontal.
Find her gravitational potential energy
relative to B. (Take g = 9.8 N kg⁻¹.)

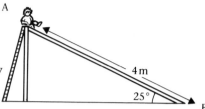

SOLUTION

Her height above B is
4 sin 25° metres.

So her PE = 20g × (4 sin 25°)
= 331.3 joules

EXERCISE 1

1 Calculate the gravitational potential energy, relative to the ground, of a
particle of mass 5 kg if it is 2 metres above the ground.

2 Calculate the gravitational potential energy, relative to the ground, of a
child of mass 30 kg sitting at the top of a slide of length 5 metres and
inclined at 36° to the horizontal.

3 A circus performer of mass 70 kg swings on a rope of length 8 metres.

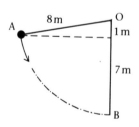

Calculate the change in his potential
energy as he moves from A to B.

4 (a) Calculate the work done by gravity (to the nearest joule) when a 50 kg
hod of bricks is carried up a ramp which has length l and is inclined at
an angle θ to the horizontal if:

(i) $l = 34.4$ metres; $\theta = 5°$ (ii) $l = 8.0$ metres; $\theta = 22°$

(b) Explain why the increase in the gravitational potential energy of the
bricks is approximately the same for each of the ramps.

5 A bricklayer carries a hod of bricks (50 kg) up a ladder. Calculate the length
of the ladder if it is inclined at 70° to the horizontal and the increase in the
gravitational PE of the bricks is 4300 J.

4.2 Conserving energy

You may have been told that 'energy cannot be created or destroyed'. This suggests that energy is conserved. Yet, when two bodies collide, unless the collision is perfectly elastic, there will be a loss of kinetic energy.

Look at the following situation.

A child (40 kg) slides down a water chute. The chute is very slippery and there is no friction to oppose motion.

The child initially travels at $3\,\mathrm{m\,s^{-1}}$, having been given a push at the start.

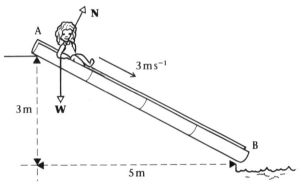

(a) How much work is done by each force acting on the child as she goes from A to B?

(b) With what speed does the child enter the water?

(c) What is the PE of the child at A? What is the KE of the child at A?

(d) What are the PE and KE of the child at B?

(e) Is energy conserved?

(f) Is energy conserved if a constant frictional force of 100 newtons opposes motion?

TASKSHEET 1 — A flying ball (page 64)

You have seen that in the absence of friction or air resistance, potential energy changes into kinetic energy (or vice versa) in such a way that the total energy is constant.

On the other hand, if friction or air resistance is present, some of the energy appears to be lost.

If gravity is the only force doing work, then it is always true that the total energy is constant.

> If the only force doing work is gravity, then at any two positions A and B:
>
> (KE + PE) at A = (KE + PE) at B

EXAMPLE 3

A marble rolls down a chute and becomes a projectile.

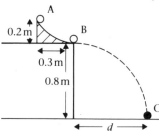

(a) Calculate its speed as it leaves the chute.

(b) The marble lands at distance d metres from the table. Calculate d.

SOLUTION

Assume that the marble is a particle of mass m kg and that there is no friction.

(a) The normal contact force is always perpendicular to the velocity and so does no work. The only force doing work is gravity, so:

$$(KE + PE) \text{ at B} = (KE + PE) \text{ at A}$$

Choose values for the potential energy relative to the level of B.
$$\tfrac{1}{2}mv^2 + 0 = 0 + mg(0.2)$$
$$\Rightarrow v = 2$$

Therefore the speed of the marble at B is $2\,\text{m}\,\text{s}^{-1}$.

> Would you obtain the same answer if you found the potential energy at each point relative to the level of C?

(b) Assume that the motion is horizontal at B.

The initial velocity is $\mathbf{u} = \begin{bmatrix} 2 \\ 0 \end{bmatrix}$. The acceleration is $\mathbf{a} = \begin{bmatrix} 0 \\ -g \end{bmatrix}$.

Since $\mathbf{u} = \begin{bmatrix} 2 \\ 0 \end{bmatrix}$, $\mathbf{v} = \begin{bmatrix} 2 \\ -gt \end{bmatrix}$

Since $\mathbf{r_B} = \begin{bmatrix} 0 \\ 0 \end{bmatrix}$, $\mathbf{r} = \begin{bmatrix} 2t \\ -\frac{1}{2}gt^2 \end{bmatrix}$

Taking $g = 10\,\mathrm{m\,s^{-2}}$, $\mathbf{r} = \begin{bmatrix} 2t \\ -5t^2 \end{bmatrix}$. At C, $\mathbf{r} = \begin{bmatrix} d \\ -0.8 \end{bmatrix}$.

$\Rightarrow d = 2t$ and $-0.8 = -5t^2$
$\Rightarrow t = 0.4$ and $d = 0.8$

EXERCISE 2

1 A squash ball of mass 20 grams is hit vertically upward with speed $15\,\mathrm{m\,s^{-1}}$.

   (a) What is its potential energy relative to its initial position when it has travelled 3 metres?

   (b) What is its speed at that point?

   (c) What is its potential energy at the highest point of its path?

2 A bob of mass 100 grams, on a string of length 1 metre, is released from rest when the string makes an angle of 80° with the vertical as shown. What is its kinetic energy at the lowest point of its path?

3 Two ball bearings (one twice as heavy as the other) can swing freely on the ends of light string as shown in the diagram. The lighter ball bearing swings down and collides with the heavier one, which has a piece of Blu-Tack on it so that the two stick together on impact.

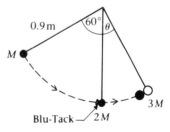

   (a) What is the speed of the lighter ball bearing just before impact?

   (b) What is the speed of the combined mass immediately after impact?

   (c) Predict the angle of swing of the combined mass.

4.3 Elastic potential energy

If you stretch a bow, the (positive) work done by the pull you apply (in the direction of displacement) will be equal and opposite to the (negative) work done by the tension in the bow. However, the tension, like gravity, does not disappear once motion stops; it has the **potential** to do positive work. Such energy is called **elastic potential energy** (abbreviated to EPE) and this is the energy which is transferred to the arrow as kinetic energy when the bow is released.

TASKSHEET 2 — Tension (page 65)

The tension in a stretched spring is proportional to the extension of the spring.

$$T = ke$$

where k is called the **spring constant**.

If a spring with spring constant k is stretched (or compressed) a distance x beyond its natural length, show that the elastic potential energy of the spring is:

$$\frac{kx^2}{2}$$

EXAMPLE 4

A spring of length 10 cm is stretched to a length of 12 cm by a pull of 10 newtons.

(a) What is its spring constant?

(b) What work must be done to stretch it a further 2 cm?

SOLUTION

(a) $T = kx$
So $10 = k \times 0.02$
$$\Rightarrow k = \frac{10}{0.02} = 500\,\mathrm{N\,m^{-1}}$$

(b) Work done to stretch the spring to 12 cm $= 500 \times \dfrac{(0.02)^2}{2} = 0.1\,\mathrm{J}$

Work done to stretch the spring to 14 cm $= 500 \times \dfrac{(0.04)^2}{2} = 0.4\,\mathrm{J}$

Work done to stretch the spring from 12 cm to 14 cm $= 0.3\,\mathrm{J}$

EXERCISE 3

1 A spring has a spring constant of $1000\,\mathrm{N\,m^{-1}}$.

(a) What is the work done if it is stretched by 50 cm?

(b) What is the work done if the spring is stretched by 150 cm?

2 The work done to stretch an elastic band by 10 cm from its natural length is 0.2 joules. What is its spring constant?

3 A spring is compressed by a distance of 5 cm. Its spring constant is $500\,\mathrm{N\,m^{-1}}$.

(a) What work has been done?

(b) What work must be done to compress it by a further 5 cm?

4.4 **Conserving mechanical energy**

Three quantities with the name 'energy' have so far been introduced: kinetic energy, gravitational potential energy and elastic potential energy. Energy, however, appears in many different forms. Heat and electricity are both forms of energy. Some substances possess energy which can be released when they undergo a chemical change; for example, when coal is burnt it releases energy in the form of heat and light. A person has a similar store of 'chemical energy' which can be released in the form of mechanical energy when movement is required.

Energy is continually changing from one form to another. When you push a pencil across the table the chemical energy you release is changed into heat energy. (The temperatures of both the table and the pencil increase due to the action of friction.) When you lift a pencil up, the chemical energy released is changed into gravitational potential energy. This can be changed into kinetic energy if the pencil is allowed to fall. Gravitational potential energy and kinetic energy are both forms of **mechanical energy**. A spring has mechanical energy when extended or compressed.

Set a mass on the end of a spring oscillating.

(a) Time one complete oscillation.

(b) Draw a rough sketch of the (time, KE) graph for one complete oscillation.

(c) Draw rough sketches of the graphs of the gravitational PE of the mass and of the elastic PE of the spring against the time for one complete oscillation.

(d) What can you say about the total mechanical energy of the system?

Many problems are very much easier to solve if you can assume that mechanical energy is conserved. While this may be a reasonable assumption in many situations, you need to check carefully that energy is not added to the system from outside and that there are no dissipative forces (such as friction) which would change the energy from mechanical energy to a different form of energy such as heat or light.

> If there are no dissipative forces, such as friction, and no energy is added from outside, then the total mechanical energy of a system is conserved.

EXAMPLE 5

A marble slides down a chute from A to B.

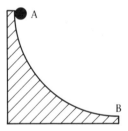

What assumptions are made if it is assumed that the decrease in PE is equal to the increase in KE?

SOLUTION

You would assume that

 (i) the chute is smooth, so there is no friction;

(ii) there is no air resistance.

There would, in practice, be some doubt about the validity of these assumptions. Although air resistance **is** likely to be negligible, the assumption of a smooth chute is unlikely to be valid and so any analysis based on this assumption must be interpreted accordingly.

> In what way would the presence of friction affect the motion of the marble?

EXAMPLE 6

A 200 gram mass is attached to the end of a spring (natural length 0.3 metre) and hangs at rest (in equilibrium). The mass is then pulled down a distance 0.15 metre (to position A) and released. The mass oscillates as shown. Assume the spring obeys Hooke's law, with spring constant $8\,\mathrm{N\,m^{-1}}$.

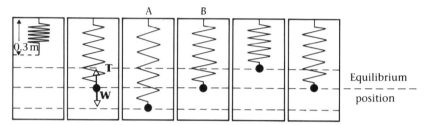

What is the resultant force acting on the mass when it is in position B and what is its velocity at that time?

SOLUTION

Position B is the equilibrium position so the resultant force is zero (i.e. the tension in the spring is equal and opposite to the gravitational pull).

> Explain why the spring is extended 0.25 m beyond its natural length when the mass is in position B.

Being in equilibrium does not mean the mass is not moving. The direction of its motion is obvious. The problem is how to calculate the magnitude of the velocity.

As no energy from outside is put into the system once it is in motion and as energy loss due to air resistance is negligible, it is reasonable to assume that the total mechanical energy of the system is constant.

(In fact, mechanical energy is gradually lost, mostly as heat. In the short term, however, this is a reasonably good model.)

Position A

KE $\quad \dfrac{mv^2}{2} = 0$

PE $\quad mgh = 0 \quad$ (relative to position A)

EPE $\quad \dfrac{kx^2}{2} = \dfrac{8 \times 0.4^2}{2}$

$= 0.64$ joules

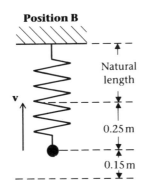

Position B

Natural
length

0.25 m

0.15 m

KE $\quad \dfrac{mv^2}{2} = \dfrac{0.2v^2}{2}$

$\quad = 0.1v^2$ joules

PE $\quad mgh = 0.2 \times 10 \times 0.15$
$\quad = 0.3$ joules

EPE $\quad \dfrac{kx^2}{2} = \dfrac{8 \times 0.25^2}{2}$

$\quad = 0.25$ joules

Total mechanical energy at A = total mechanical energy at B
$$0.64 = 0.1v^2 + 0.3 + 0.25$$
$\Rightarrow \qquad\qquad\qquad 0.9 = v^2$
The velocity of the mass is $0.95 \, \text{m s}^{-1}$.

EXERCISE 4

1 A light spring, of natural length 0.2 metre, is extended to a length of 0.3 metre when a mass of 100 grams is hung on it. It is then pulled down a further 0.1 metre and released.

(a) Find the velocity of the mass when the spring next has length 0.3 metre.

(b) Where is its elastic potential energy greatest?

2 A mass of 2 kg is hung from a spring with spring constant $500 \, \text{N m}^{-1}$.

(a) Find the extension when the mass hangs in equilibrium.

(b) The mass is pulled down until the extension is 0.1 metre and then released. Find the speed of the mass when the spring reaches its unstretched length.

3

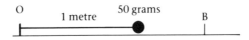

O
1 metre
50 grams
B

The diagram shows a mass of 50 grams lying on a smooth table. It is fixed to point O by an elastic string of length 1 metre. It is held at point B by a force of 4 newtons and then released. OB is 1.5 metres.

At what speed is the mass travelling when it passes O?

4 A stunt actor attaches one end of a nylon rope to himself and the other end to an anchor point on the edge of the roof of a high-rise building. He then steps off the roof and falls vertically. The actor has mass 76 kg and the roof is 200 metres above ground. The rope has unstretched length 100 metres and its tension, T newtons, when stretched by a further x metres, is given by the formula:

$$T = 30x$$

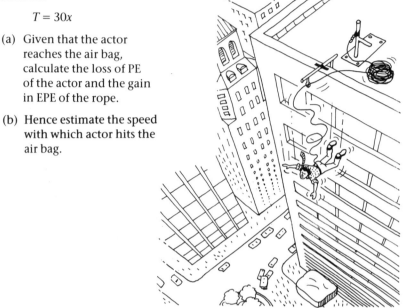

(a) Given that the actor reaches the air bag, calculate the loss of PE of the actor and the gain in EPE of the rope.

(b) Hence estimate the speed with which actor hits the air bag.

5 A child's toy rocket (mass 20 grams) is fired by releasing a compressed spring. The natural length of the spring is 5 cm, the compressed length is 1 cm and the spring constant is $1000\,\mathrm{N\,m^{-1}}$.

Estimate the height the rocket will reach when fired vertically up in the air.

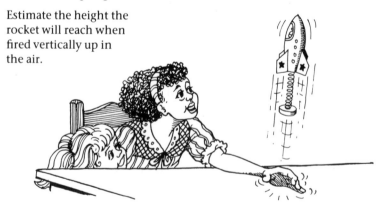

After working through this chapter you should:

1 know that the gravitational potential energy (PE) of a body is always measured relative to an arbitrary fixed reference position (it is defined as the work that would be done by gravity if the body were to move from its present position to the fixed reference position);

2 know that a particle of mass m kg, at a height h metres above the floor, has gravitational potential energy mgh joules relative to the floor;

3 know that if gravity is the only force doing work then, at any two positions A and B:

$$(KE + PE) \text{ at A} = (KE + PE) \text{ at B}$$

4 know that if a spring, with spring constant k, is stretched or compressed a distance x metres beyond its natural length, then its elastic potential energy (EPE) is $\dfrac{kx^2}{2}$ joules;

5 know that if there are no dissipative forces, such as friction, and no energy is added from outside, then the total mechanical energy of a system is conserved;

6 know that kinetic energy, gravitational potential energy and elastic potential energy are all forms of mechanical energy.

A flying ball

A snooker ball of mass 50 grams is thrown vertically upwards with a speed of $10\,\text{m}\,\text{s}^{-1}$. Assuming that there is no air resistance and that $g = 10\,\text{N}\,\text{kg}^{-1}$, make a table of its kinetic and potential energies as it rises.

Height above point of projection (metres)	KE (joules)	PE relative to point of projection (joules)
0		
1		
2		
3 etc.		

1 How high does it rise?

2 State the sum of the potential and kinetic energies at each height. Is energy conserved?

3 Describe (in words) how kinetic energy and potential energy vary as the ball rises.

4 If, instead of a snooker ball, a tennis ball of the same mass is used, what difference will this make?

Assume that the resistance to motion is a constant 0.125 newton due to air resistance and draw up a similar table including a column for the sum of the kinetic and potential energies.

5 Is energy conserved in this case?
What has happened to the energy?

Tension

2

You will need: Retort stand or clamp
Spring
Ruler
Mass holder and masses
Stop-watch

Hooke's experimental law states that the tension in a stretched spring is proportional to the extension of the spring beyond its natural length. (The constant of proportionality is called the **spring constant**.)

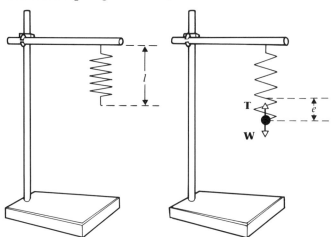

When the mass hangs at rest (equilibrium), the tension in the spring, T, is equal and opposite to the weight, W, of the mass.

Hooke's law states that:

$$T = ke$$

1 Place various masses on the mass holder, record the extension of the spring in each case, and hence draw the (extension, tension) graph for the spring.

2 Use your graph to estimate k, the spring constant for your spring.

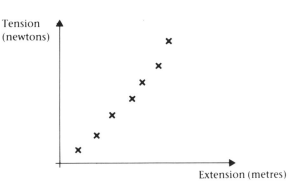

5 Modelling circular motion

5.1 Changing speed, changing energy

In chapter 1 you looked at some examples of bodies in horizontal circular motion – the chair-o-plane, conical pendulum, rotor, cyclist on a circular track – and in each case the speed was assumed to be constant. By contrast, when bodies move in a vertical circle their speed may change continually.

For example:

A conker on a string.

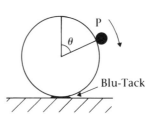

A marble rolling on the surface of a cylinder.

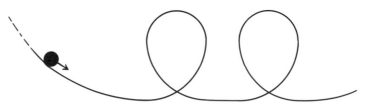

A marble rolling on a loop-the-loop track.

(a) In which of the situations above is it reasonable to assume conservation of energy?

(b) Describe what happens to the kinetic and potential energies of the marble as it moves along the track.

(c) How would using a toy car rather than a marble affect what happens?

Set up the apparatus to validate your conjectures.

When tackling the more complicated problems in circular motion, an important principle to use is the conservation of mechanical energy. This is illustrated in the following example.

E X A M P L E   1

A marble is released from rest at A and loops the loop.

Calculate its speed on reaching:

(a) the lowest point B of the loop;

(b) the highest point D;

(c) the general point P, where angle BOP = θ.

What have you assumed?

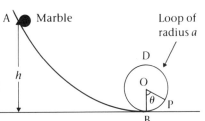

S O L U T I O N

Some assumptions are:

● the rotational energy of the marble is ignored;

● the marble can be modelled as a particle of mass m kg;

● energy is conserved (i.e. resistance is ignored);

● the initial speed is zero;

● the height of h is sufficient for the marble to reach D;

● the gravitational force per unit mass is $10\,\text{N}\,\text{kg}^{-1}$.

(a) At B: $10\not mh = \frac{1}{2}\not mv^2 - \frac{1}{2}\not mu^2$
$$v^2 = 20h$$
$$v = \surd(20h)$$

(b) At D: $10\not mh = \frac{1}{2}\not mv^2 + 10\not m \times 2a$
$$v^2 = 20h - 40a$$
$$v = \surd(20(h - 2a))$$

(c) At P: $10mh = \frac{1}{2}mv^2 + 10m(a - a\cos\theta)$
$$v^2 = 20h - 20a(1 - \cos\theta)$$
$$v = \surd(20(h - a + a\cos\theta))$$

For a gravitational force per unit mass of $g\,\text{N}\,\text{kg}^{-1}$, the velocity at the general point P is given by:

$$v = \surd(2g(h - a + a\cos\theta))$$

5.2 Acceleration

When solving real problems in circular motion the energy equation is usually insufficient. You must, in addition, consider the forces acting and apply Newton's second law, $\mathbf{F} = m\mathbf{a}$.

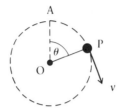

A conker of mass m on the end of a string moves in a vertical circle of radius r.

At time t, its speed is v and angle $AOP = \theta$.

(a) What forces are acting on the conker?

(b) Does the resultant force act towards the centre of circular motion?

The tasksheet will show you how to analyse the motion of the conker and enable you to deduce some useful general results about acceleration and circular motion.

TASKSHEET 1 — Calculating acceleration (page 78)

When the motion of an object follows a circular path, its acceleration has two components, radial and tangential.

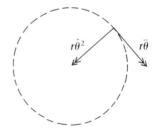

The radial component has magnitude $r\dot{\theta}^2 = r\omega^2 = \dfrac{v^2}{r}$.

The tangential component has magnitude $r\ddot{\theta} = r\dot{\omega}$.

The tangential component will be new to you, but the radial component should be familiar from your work with horizontal circular motion at a constant angular speed.

EXAMPLE 2

A 2 kg mass is connected to a point A by a light string. The string is 1.2 metres long and has a breaking strain of 50 newtons.

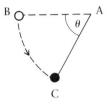

The mass is released from the point B, where AB is horizontal and of length 1.2 metres. The string breaks when the mass reaches point C.

Find the angle θ.

SOLUTION

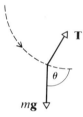

There are just two forces acting on the mass if air resistance is taken as being negligible.

By Newton's second law,

$$\text{tangentially:} \qquad mg \cos \theta = mr\dot{\omega}$$

$$\text{radially:} \qquad T - mg \sin \theta = \frac{mv^2}{r}$$

By conservation of mechanical energy:

$$mgr \sin \theta = \frac{1}{2}mv^2$$

$$T - mg \sin \theta = \frac{mv^2}{r}$$

$\Rightarrow \qquad\qquad\qquad T - mg \sin \theta = 2mg \sin \theta$

$\Rightarrow \qquad\qquad\qquad\qquad\qquad T = 3mg \sin \theta$

Assuming $T = 50\,\text{N}, \quad m = 2\,\text{kg}$ and $g = 10\,\text{N kg}^{-1}$

$\Rightarrow \qquad\qquad\qquad\qquad\qquad 50 = 60 \sin \theta$

$\Rightarrow \qquad\qquad\qquad\qquad\qquad \theta = 56.4°$

Would your answer be different if the string was only 0.6 metre long?

Notice that the equation for the tangential component of force was not needed to obtain a solution. When solving problems on vertical circular motion, you will find that it is often sufficient to use:

• the energy equation;

• Newton's second law in the radially inward direction.

EXAMPLE 3

A girl of mass 30 kg is sitting on a swing. The ropes of the swing are 2 metres long and they make an angle of 30° with the horizontal when she reaches the top point of her swing. Find:

(a) the greatest tension in the ropes;

(b) the greatest speed of the girl.

SOLUTION

Assume the girl is a particle on the end of a light string of length 2 metres. Let $g = 10 \text{N kg}^{-1}$ and let the tension in the string be T newtons.

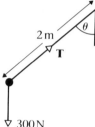

Using Newton's second law radially,

$$T - 300 \cos \theta = 30a$$

But $a = \dfrac{v^2}{r} = \dfrac{v^2}{2}$

$$\Rightarrow \quad T - 300 \cos \theta = 15v^2 \quad \text{①}$$

By conservation of energy,

$$\frac{1}{2}\cancel{m}v^2 = \cancel{m}g(2 \cos \theta - 1)$$

$$v^2 = 20(2 \cos \theta - 1)$$

Substitute in ①

$$T = 300\,(2 \cos \theta - 1) + 300 \cos \theta$$
$$= 900 \cos \theta - 300$$

So T is greatest when $\theta = 0°$,

$$T_{\max} = 600 \text{N}$$

The greatest speed of the girl is when her PE is least, i.e. at the bottom of the swing.

$$v^2 = 20\,(2 \cos \theta - 1)$$
$$= 20$$
$$v = 2\sqrt{5}\,\text{m s}^{-1}$$

EXERCISE 1

1   A girl is skateboarding on a rink which is the shape of a bowl whose cross-section is given below.

2 metres   2 metres

She has mass 40 kg and her maximum speed is $5\,\mathrm{m\,s^{-1}}$.

(a) How high up the slope can she go?

(b) What is the reaction between the skateboarder and the skateboard at this point?

2   A small boy of mass 40 kg holds on to the end of a rope in the gym and jumps off a bar. The length of the rope is 5 metres and the height of the bar is 4 metres below the point of suspension of the rope. Find:

(a) the speed of the boy at the bottom of his swing;

(b) the tension in the rope at the bottom of his swing;

(c) the tension in the rope when he reaches the highest point at the other end of his swing.

3   A girl swings a conker around in a vertical circle. The conker has mass 10 grams and its velocity is $3\,\mathrm{m\,s^{-1}}$ downwards when the string is horizontal. The string is 50 cm long and the conker hits another when it makes an angle of 120° with the upward vertical. Find:

(a) the conker's velocity at this point;

(b) the tension in the string at this point.

5.3 Losing contact

When a marble is released from rest at some position, A, on the approach track to a loop-the-loop, it will do one of three things; oscillate to and fro about B, loop the loop or lose contact with the track at some position between C and D.

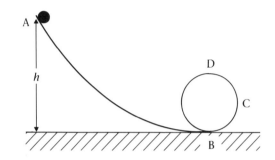

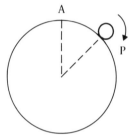

Similarly, in the case of the marble rolling around the perimeter of a cylinder, a position P is reached at which the marble loses contact.

(a) What forces act on the marble as it moves along the track/cylinder?

(b) What is the condition for the marble to lose contact with the track/cylinder?

Once the marble loses contact with the track/cylinder it becomes a projectile and it is of interest to know where contact is lost and where the marble lands.

TASKSHEET 2 – The skier (page 79)

On the tasksheet, you considered the problem of where the marble loses contact with the cylinder. The problem of analysing the motion of the marble on the track is left as a possible investigation.

5.4 Investigations

The following are examples of suitable topics for circular motion investigations.

(a) The chair-o-plane

Problem · What happens as the speed increases?
Do empty chairs swing out as far as full ones?

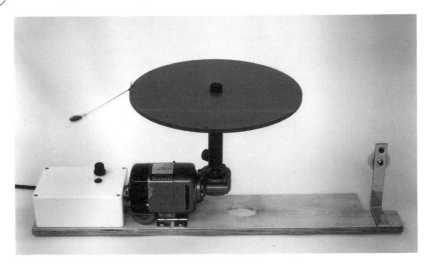

(b) The loop-the-loop

Problem   What is the critical height for looping the loop?

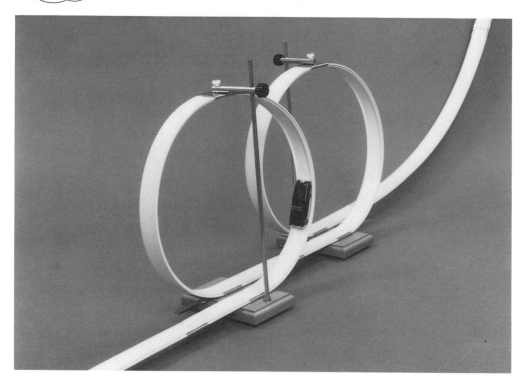

(c) The longboat

Problem What is the force at the support?

A simple pendulum provides an initial model.

(d) The rotor

This is a model of the rotor at Wicksteed Park.

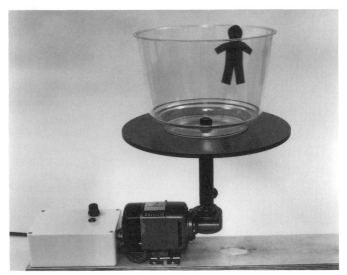

Problem What is the critical speed above which the floor can be removed?

(e) The beast

Pennies rotating on
a banked track provide
a simple model of the
Alton beast.

  Why is the track banked on the bends?
What is the best banking angle?

(f) The thunder-looper

Problem

The loop is best modelled as three segments of a circle, two quarter circles of radius $2r$ each at the bottom, joined by a semicircle of radius r at the top.

What effect does this have on the ride?

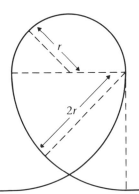

After working through this chapter you should:

1   know that when a body moves in a vertical circle, its speed is not necessarily constant;

2   know that when the motion of an object follows a circular path, its acceleration has two components, radial and tangential. The radial component has magnitude $r\omega^2$ towards the centre of the circle; the tangential component has magnitude $r\dot{\omega}$.

3   know that if gravity is the only force doing work on a particle travelling in a vertical circle, then the velocity at any point can be found by using the principle of conservation of mechanical energy;

4   know how to model real situations involving circular motion.

Calculating acceleration

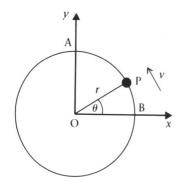

A particle moves in a vertical circle of radius r. (It could represent a conker on a string or a marble rolling on the outside of a cylinder.) At time t, its speed is v and angle POB = θ. Its angular speed is the rate of change of θ, $\dfrac{d\theta}{dt}$.

A useful notation is to write $\dot{\theta}$ for $\dfrac{d\theta}{dt}$ and

$\ddot{\theta}$ for $\dfrac{d^2\theta}{dt^2}$.

1   Show that $\begin{bmatrix} \cos \theta \\ \sin \theta \end{bmatrix}$ is a unit vector in the direction $\overrightarrow{OP}$.

2   With respect to the (x, y) axes shown in the diagram, the displacement $\overrightarrow{OP}$ is given by:

$$\mathbf{r} = r \begin{bmatrix} \cos \theta \\ \sin \theta \end{bmatrix}$$

Find the velocity $\mathbf{v}$ and show that its magnitude is $r\dot{\theta}$.

3   (a) Show that the acceleration is given by:

$$\mathbf{a} = -r\dot{\theta}^2 \begin{bmatrix} \cos \theta \\ \sin \theta \end{bmatrix} + r\ddot{\theta} \begin{bmatrix} -\sin \theta \\ \cos \theta \end{bmatrix}$$

   (b) Show that $\begin{bmatrix} -\sin \theta \\ \cos \theta \end{bmatrix}$ is a unit vector in a direction perpendicular to $\overrightarrow{OP}$.

   (Hint: use the scalar product.)

   (c) Show that the component of acceleration in the direction $\overrightarrow{PO}$ has magnitude $\dfrac{v^2}{r}$.

The skier

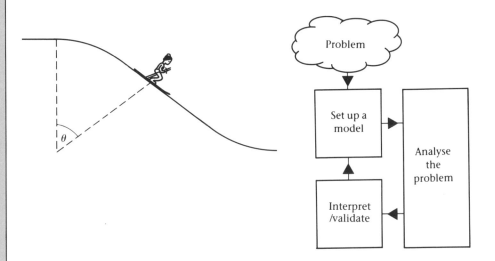

Starting from rest on the horizontal, a skier travelling down a convex slope picks up speed as she moves downhill and may take off into the air at some position.

Her motion might be modelled by a marble rolling around the outside of a cylinder, for example, a cake tin, fixed to a table with Blu-Tack.

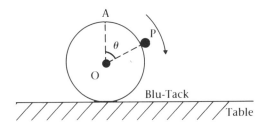

 To find θ at the take-off position.

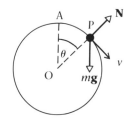

Set up a model

Set up a simple model in which the effect of friction is ignored.

Assume that the skier (marble) is a particle of mass m, sliding on a smooth surface.

1 What other assumptions should you make?

Analyse the problem

If friction can be ignored, you can apply the energy equation:

total energy at A = total energy at P
(PE + KE)   (PE + KE)

$$mg2a + 0 = mga(1 + \cos \theta) + \frac{1}{2}mv^2$$

$$\Rightarrow v^2 = 2ga(1 - \cos \theta) \quad \text{①}$$

By Newton's second law, $F = ma$ in the direction PO gives:

$$mg \cos \theta - N = \frac{mv^2}{a}$$

When the particle loses contact with the surface, $N = 0$ and so:

$$v^2 = ga \cos \theta \quad \text{②}$$

2 Use equations ① and ② to show that: $\theta = \cos^{-1}\left(\frac{2}{3}\right)$

Interpret

3 Explain why the marble leaves the surface at a distance $\frac{a}{3}$ below A.

Validate

Validation can be achieved by coating the cylinder with talcum powder and measuring the length, s, of the arc from A to the take-off position; $\frac{s}{a}$ gives θ.

4E Determine where the marble should land on the table.

Solutions

1 Circular motion

1.1 Modelling horizontal circular motion

1 $v = 120 \, \text{km} \, \text{h}^{-1} = \dfrac{120 \times 1000}{3600} = 33.\dot{3} \, \text{m} \, \text{s}^{-1}$

$a = \dfrac{v^2}{r}$

So $30 = \dfrac{33.3^2}{r} \Rightarrow r = 37.0$ metres

2   Newton's second law gives:

$$\begin{bmatrix} T\sin\theta \\ T\cos\theta \end{bmatrix} + \begin{bmatrix} 0 \\ -0.5g \end{bmatrix} = \begin{bmatrix} 0.5 \times \dfrac{v^2}{0.3} \\ 0 \end{bmatrix}$$

$\sin\theta = \dfrac{0.3}{0.8} \Rightarrow \theta = 22.02°$

$T\cos 22.02° = 0.5 \times 9.8 \Rightarrow T = 5.29$ newtons

$5.28 \sin 22.02° = 0.5 \times \dfrac{v^2}{0.3} \Rightarrow v = 1.09 \, \text{m} \, \text{s}^{-1}$

3   Newton's second law gives:

$$\begin{bmatrix} T\sin\theta \\ T\cos\theta \end{bmatrix} + \begin{bmatrix} 0 \\ -4g \end{bmatrix} = \begin{bmatrix} 4r\omega^2 \\ 0 \end{bmatrix}$$

$T\sin\theta = 4r\omega^2$
but $\sin\theta = r \Rightarrow T = 4\omega^2$
$4\omega^2 < 60 \Rightarrow \omega < 3.87 \, \text{rad} \, \text{s}^{-1}$
$T\cos\theta = 4g \Rightarrow \cos\theta = \dfrac{39.2}{T}$

$\Rightarrow \cos\theta > \dfrac{39.2}{60}$

$\theta < 49.2°$

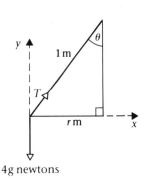

4 Newton's second law gives:

$$\begin{bmatrix} N \\ F \end{bmatrix} + \begin{bmatrix} 0 \\ -75g \end{bmatrix} = \begin{bmatrix} 375\omega^2 \\ 0 \end{bmatrix}$$

$\Rightarrow F = 75g = 735$ newtons

but $F = \dfrac{2}{5}N \quad \Rightarrow N = 1837.5$ newtons

$375\omega^2 = 1837.5 \Rightarrow \omega = 2.21\,\text{rad}\,\text{s}^{-1}$

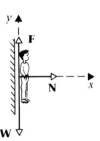

5 Newton's second law gives:

$$\begin{bmatrix} -R\sin 30° \\ R\cos 30° \end{bmatrix} + \begin{bmatrix} 0 \\ -100g \end{bmatrix} = \begin{bmatrix} -100 \times \dfrac{v^2}{10} \\ 0 \end{bmatrix}$$

$R = \dfrac{100g}{\cos 30°} \Rightarrow R = 1131.6$ newtons

$1131.6 \sin 30° = 10v^2 \Rightarrow v = 7.52\,\text{m}\,\text{s}^{-1}$

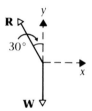

2 Work and kinetic energy

2.1 Areas under graphs

EXERCISE 1

1 The change in momentum is $\dfrac{90}{1000} \times 8 + \dfrac{90}{1000} \times 6 = 1.26\,\text{Ns}$

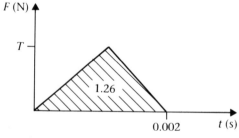

The maximum force T satisfies:

$T \times 0.001 = 1.26$

$\Rightarrow T = 1260$ newtons

2   Using the trapezium rule, the total impulse is approximately:

$$10 \times (850 + 565 + 370 + 215 + 150 + 105) = 22\,550\,\text{Ns}$$

The final speed is therefore $22.55\,\text{m s}^{-1}$.

3   Initial momentum $= \begin{bmatrix} 4 \\ 2 \end{bmatrix}$

Final momentum $= \begin{bmatrix} 2 \\ 3 \end{bmatrix}$

Impulse = change in momentum

$$= \begin{bmatrix} -2 \\ 1 \end{bmatrix} \text{kg m s}^{-1}$$

4   (a) $\displaystyle\int_0^{0.5} 42\,000 \sin (2\pi t) \, \text{d}t \approx 13\,400\,\text{Ns}$

(b) The force is perpendicular to the barrier and so the change in momentum must also be perpendicular to the barrier.

(c) $1200 \times 20 = 24\,000\,\text{Ns}$ at $30°$ to the barrier.

(d)

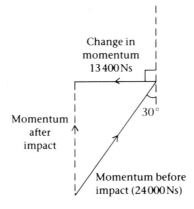

A scale drawing shows that the momentum after impact is approximately $21\,000\,\text{Ns}$ at $4°$ to the barrier.

(e) The velocity is approximately $18\,\text{m s}^{-1}$ at $4°$ to the barrier.

2.2   Speed and distance

Find the distance covered, x, in terms of u, v and t.

Use the equation $Ft = mv - mu$ to obtain the expression:

$$Fx = \tfrac{1}{2}mv^2 - \tfrac{1}{2}mu^2$$

for the product, force × distance.

$$x = \frac{u + v}{2} t$$

So $\quad Fx = Ft \dfrac{u + v}{2}$

$$= (mv - mu) \frac{u + v}{2}$$

$$= \frac{1}{2}mv^2 - \frac{1}{2}mu^2$$

> What is the kinetic energy, in joules, of a 1 kg mass travelling with a speed of $1\,\mathrm{m\,s^{-1}}$?

$$\frac{1}{2} \times 1 \times 1^2 = \frac{1}{2} \mathrm{J}$$

> Why is the force negative?

You may have realised that this is because the force is in the opposite direction to the direction of the motion. A general extension of the work and energy equation to cases where the force and motion are not in the same direction requires a vectorial treatment. This will be considered later.

EXERCISE 2

1   The kinetic energy $\dfrac{1}{2}mv^2 = \dfrac{1}{2} \times 1500 \times \left(150 \times \dfrac{1000}{3600} \right)^2 \mathrm{J} = 1.3 \times 10^6\,\mathrm{J}$

The retarding force, F newtons, is given by:

$$F \times 100 = \frac{1}{2} \times 1500 \times 0^2 - 1.3 \times 10^6$$
$$\Rightarrow F = -1.3 \times 10^4$$

The retarding force has magnitude 1.3×10^4 newtons.

2   The resistive force, F newtons, is given by:

$$F \times 0.02 = \frac{1}{2} \times 0.015 \times 300^2 - \frac{1}{2} \times 0.015 \times 500^2$$
$$\Rightarrow F = -6 \times 10^4$$

The resistive force has magnitude 6×10^4 newtons.

3   The accelerating force, *F* newtons, is given by:

$$F \times 15 = 1000 \times 108 \times \frac{1000}{3600}$$
$$\Rightarrow F = 2000$$

The accelerating force is 2000 newtons.

The distance travelled while accelerating, *x* metres, is given by:

$$2000x = \frac{1}{2} \times 1000 \times \left(108 \times \frac{1000}{3600}\right)^2$$
$$\Rightarrow x = 225$$

The distance travelled while slowing down, *y* metres, is given by:

$$-500y = \frac{1}{2} \times 1000 \times 0^2 - \frac{1}{2} \times 1000 \times \left(108 \times \frac{1000}{3600}\right)^2$$
$$\Rightarrow y = 900$$

The total distance travelled is $(225 + 900) = 1125$ metres.

4   The total work done while accelerating is:

$$(3100 \times 10 + 2000 \times 20 + 1500 \times 30 + 1100 \times 40) = 160000\,\text{J}$$

The speed attained, $v\,\text{m s}^{-1}$, is given by:

$$160000 = \frac{1}{2} \times 800 \times v^2$$
$$\Rightarrow v = 20$$

The speed attained is $20\,\text{m s}^{-1}$. In reality, the force would vary in each gear.

5 $50\,\text{km h}^{-1} = 50 \times \frac{1000}{3600}\text{m s}^{-1} = 13.89\,\text{m s}^{-1}$

The initial sliding speed of the van, $u\,\text{m s}^{-1}$, is given by:

$$-2 \times 10^4 \times 32 = \frac{1}{2} \times 2250 \times 13.89^2 - \frac{1}{2} \times 2250 \times u^2$$
$$\Rightarrow u = 27.6$$

The initial sliding speed of the van was around $27.6\,\text{m s}^{-1}$

$$27.6 \times \frac{3600}{1000} = 99.4\,\text{km h}^{-1}$$

The type of skid test described would be extremely unreliable and potentially inaccurate.

6 Circumference of (assumed circular) orbit $= 2 \times \pi \times 1.5 \times 10^8 \times 10^3$ metres
$$= 3\pi \times 10^{11} \text{ metres}$$

Speed of the Earth relative to the Sun $= \dfrac{3\pi \times 10^{11}}{365 \times 24 \times 60 \times 60} \text{m s}^{-1}$

$$\approx 29.9 \times 10^3 \text{m s}^{-1}$$

Kinetic energy of the Earth $= \dfrac{1}{2} \times 6.04 \times 10^{24} \times 29.9^2 \times 10^6 \text{J}$

$$\approx 3 \times 10^{33} \text{J (to 1 s.f.)}$$

2.3 Work done by a variable force

EXERCISE 3

1

Distance (m)	0		1		2		3		4		5		6		7	
Force (N)	400		300		240		210		190		160		130		80	
Average force over interval (N)		350		270		225		200		175		145		105		40
Kinetic energy* (J)		350		620		845		1045		1220		1365		1470		1
Velocity(m s^{-1})		8.4		11.1		13.0		14.5		15.6		16.5		17.1		1

* For instance, the energy after 2 m is $(350 \times 1 + 270 \times 1)$ J.

2 Kinetic energy acquired $= \displaystyle\int_0^{50} (4000 - 22.5x - 0.25x^2)dx \text{ J}$

$$= \left[4000x - \frac{22.5x^2}{2} - \frac{0.25x^3}{3} \right]_0^{50} \text{J}$$

$$= 161\,500 \text{J}$$

Speed, $v\,\text{m s}^{-1}$, is given by:

$$161\,500 = \frac{1}{2} \times 1400 \times v^2$$

$$\Rightarrow v = 15.2$$

After 50 metres, the van is travelling at $15\,\text{m s}^{-1}$ (about $55\,\text{km h}^{-1}$).

3

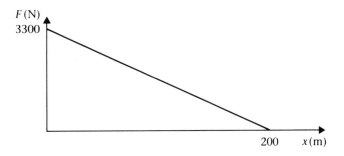

The (distance, force) graph is as shown. The kinetic energy acquired equals the area under this graph over the appropriate interval.

By inspection, $F = 3300 - \dfrac{3300x}{200} = 3300 - 16.5x$

The kinetic energy (J) acquired during the first x metres is:

$$\int_0^x (3300 - 16.5x)\, \mathrm{d}x = 3300x - 8.25x^2$$

Distance (m)	0	50	100	150	200
Kinetic energy (J)	0	144 400	247 500	309 400	330 000
Speed ($\mathrm{m\,s^{-1}}$)	0	17.0*	22.2	24.9	25.7

$*144\,400 = \dfrac{1}{2} \times 1000 \times v^2$ gives $v = 17.0$

The shape of the (distance, speed) graph is:

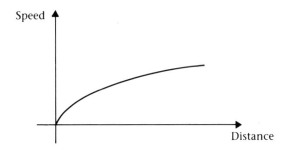

4

$mgt = mv - mu$

$\Rightarrow 30\cancel{m} = \cancel{m}v$

$v = 30\,\mathrm{m\,s^{-1}}$

$\cancel{m}gh = \dfrac{1}{2}\cancel{m}v^2 - \dfrac{1}{2}\cancel{m}u^2$

$\Rightarrow 10h = 450$

$h = 45$ metres

87

2.4 Collisions

E X E R C I S E 4

1

	Before collision	**After collision**

(a)　(i) *mu*　　　　　　　　　　　　　*mu*

(ii) $\frac{1}{2}mu^2$　　　　　　　$\frac{1}{2}mu^2$

(iii) speed of approach = *u*　　speed of separation = *u*

(b)　(i) 2*mu*　　　　　　　$\frac{2}{3}mu + \frac{4}{3}mu = 2mu$

(ii) *mu²*　　　　　　　$\frac{1}{9}mu^2 + \frac{8}{9}mu^2 = mu^2$

(iii) speed of approach = *u*　　speed of separation $= \frac{4}{3}u - \frac{1}{3}u = u$

(c)　(i) *mu*　　　　　　　$-\frac{1}{3}mu + \frac{4}{3}mu = mu$

(ii) $\frac{1}{2}mu^2$　　　　$\frac{1}{18}mu^2 + \frac{4}{9}mu^2 = \frac{1}{2}mu^2$

(iii) speed of approach = *u*　　speed of separation $= \frac{2}{3}u - \left(-\frac{1}{3}u\right) = u$

Before collision

2　(a)　Let the speed of one truck after the collision be *w*.

$m \rightarrow v$　$v \leftarrow m$

After collision

speed of separation = speed of approach
= 2*v*

$m \rightarrow w$　　$m \rightarrow w + 2v$

So the speed of the other truck after the collision is *w* + 2*v*.

Since momentum is conserved, *mv* − *mv* = *mw* + *m*(*w* + 2*v*)
⇒ 0 = *w* + *w* + 2*v*
⇒ *w* = −*v*
⇒ *w* + 2*v* = −*v* + 2*v* = *v*

The velocities of the two trucks after collision are as shown.　$v \leftarrow m$　$m \rightarrow v$

The speed of each truck is *v*.

(b) Speed of approach = $3v$

   $\Rightarrow$ speed of separation = $3v$

Before collision

$\boxed{m} \!\!\mapsto 2v \quad v\!\leftarrow\! \boxed{m}$

So after collision, the trucks have speeds w and $w + 3v$.

After collision

$\boxed{m} \!\!\mapsto w \qquad \boxed{m} \!\!\mapsto w + 3v$

By conservation of momentum,

$$mv - 2mv = mw + mw + 3mv$$
$$\Rightarrow w = -2v$$

So the velocities are $-2v$ and v.

(c) In (a), the total kinetic energy before the collision is:

$$\tfrac{1}{2}mv^2 + \tfrac{1}{2}mv^2 = mv^2$$

Since the speed of each truck is unaltered after the collision, the total kinetic energy after the collision is mv^2 also.

In (b), the total kinetic energy before the collision is:

$$\tfrac{1}{2}m(2v)^2 + \tfrac{1}{2}m(v)^2 = 2mv^2 + \tfrac{1}{2}mv^2 = 2\tfrac{1}{2}mv^2$$

Since the speed of each truck is unchanged by the collision, the total kinetic energy after the collision is $2\tfrac{1}{2}mv^2$ also.

3 Using scalar products

3.1 Work done in two dimensions

> If its initial velocity is $\begin{bmatrix} u \\ 0 \end{bmatrix}$ explain why:
>
> (a) $\mathbf{v} = \begin{bmatrix} u \\ -gt \end{bmatrix}$ (b) $\mathbf{r} = \begin{bmatrix} ut \\ -\tfrac{1}{2}gt^2 \end{bmatrix}$

The only force acting is gravity and so $\dfrac{d\mathbf{v}}{dt} = \begin{bmatrix} 0 \\ -g \end{bmatrix}$.

So, $\mathbf{v} = \begin{bmatrix} u \\ 0 \end{bmatrix} + \begin{bmatrix} 0 \\ -gt \end{bmatrix} = \begin{bmatrix} u \\ -gt \end{bmatrix}$, by integration.

Similarly, $\mathbf{r} = \begin{bmatrix} 0 \\ 0 \end{bmatrix} + \begin{bmatrix} ut \\ -\tfrac{1}{2}gt^2 \end{bmatrix}$,   since $\mathbf{r} = \begin{bmatrix} 0 \\ 0 \end{bmatrix}$ when $t = 0$

EXERCISE 1

1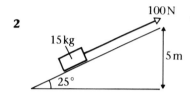

Gravitational force (weight) = 750N
Work done by this force = 750 × 35 cos 55°
= 15 056 J

2

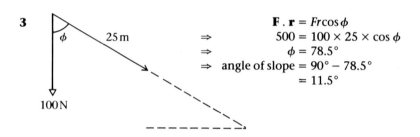

Work done by tension = 100 cos 65° × 5
= 211 J

3

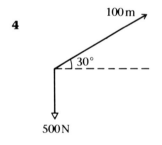

$$\mathbf{F} \cdot \mathbf{r} = Fr \cos \phi$$
$$\Rightarrow \quad 500 = 100 \times 25 \times \cos \phi$$
$$\Rightarrow \quad \phi = 78.5°$$
$$\Rightarrow \quad \text{angle of slope} = 90° - 78.5°$$
$$= 11.5°$$

4

100 m

30°

500 N

$$\mathbf{F} \cdot \mathbf{r} = Fr \cos 120°$$
$$= 500 \times 100 \times \cos 120°$$
$$= -25 000 J$$
Work done against gravity is 25 000 J

3.2 The scalar product

EXERCISE 2

1 (a) Work done = 5 × 4 × cos 60° = 10 J

(b)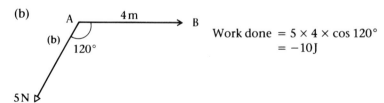

Work done = 5 × 4 × cos 120°
= −10 J

2 (a) Scalar product = $8 \times 3 \times \cos 64°$
$= 10.5$

(b) Scalar product = $2 \times 9 \times \cos 155°$
$= -16.3$

(c)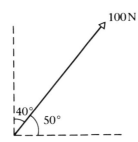

Scalar product = $2 \times 9 \times \cos 155°$
$= -16.3$

3

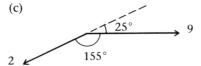

(a) Work done = $100 \cos 50° \times 7$
$= 450 \text{J}$

(b) Work done = 450J

4

Work done = $200 \cos 20° \times 1000$
$= 187939 \text{J}$
or approximately 188kJ

3.3   Using column vectors

What is the work done when a force $\mathbf{F} = \begin{bmatrix} 3 \\ 3 \end{bmatrix}$ newtons moves its

point of application through a displacement $\mathbf{r} = \begin{bmatrix} 0 \\ 4 \end{bmatrix}$ metres?

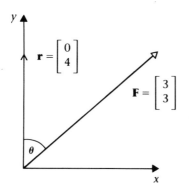

$F = \sqrt{(9 + 9)}, \quad r = 4, \quad \theta = 45°$
$\sqrt{18} \times 4 \times \cos 45° = 12 \text{Nm}$

EXERCISE 3

1 (a) $\mathbf{F} \cdot \mathbf{r} = 24 - 16 = 8\text{J}$

(b) $\mathbf{F} \cdot \mathbf{r} = -3 - 8 = -11\text{J}$

2 Force $= \begin{bmatrix} 3 \\ -5 \end{bmatrix}$, displacement $= \begin{bmatrix} 5a \\ 12a \end{bmatrix}$

$\Rightarrow 90 = \begin{bmatrix} 3 \\ -5 \end{bmatrix} \cdot \begin{bmatrix} 5a \\ 12a \end{bmatrix} = 15a - 60a$

$\Rightarrow 90 = -45a$

$\Rightarrow a = -2$

The displacement is $\begin{bmatrix} -10 \\ -24 \end{bmatrix}$ and the distance travelled is 26 metres.

3 Resultant $= \begin{bmatrix} 12 \\ 12 \end{bmatrix}$, displacement $= \begin{bmatrix} 12a \\ 12a \end{bmatrix}$

$120 = 144a + 144a$

$\Rightarrow a = \dfrac{5}{12}$

The displacement is $\begin{bmatrix} 5 \\ 5 \end{bmatrix}$ metres.

4 Taking axes along and perpendicular to the slope:

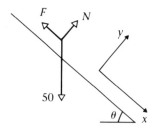

(a) Force due to gravity $= \begin{bmatrix} 50 \times \frac{3}{5} \\ -50 \times \frac{4}{5} \end{bmatrix} = \begin{bmatrix} 30 \\ -40 \end{bmatrix}$ newtons

Work done $= \begin{bmatrix} 30 \\ -40 \end{bmatrix} \cdot \begin{bmatrix} 12 \\ 0 \end{bmatrix} = 360\text{J}$

(b) Normal contact force $= \begin{bmatrix} 0 \\ N \end{bmatrix}$

Work done $= \begin{bmatrix} 0 \\ N \end{bmatrix} \cdot \begin{bmatrix} 12 \\ 0 \end{bmatrix} = 0\text{J}$

5 Diagram (a) is correct.

The angle marked θ in diagram (b) is not the angle between the force and the displacement.

3.4 Work done by several forces

E X E R C I S E 4

1 Assume there is no friction.

(a) Work done from A to B = $800 \times 5 = 4000\,$J
Work done from B to C = $800 \times 10 = 8000\,$J
Work done from C to D = $800 \times 2 = 1600\,$J

(b) Total work done = $4000 + 8000 + 1600$
$$= 13\,600\,\text{J}$$

(c) Since the initial velocity is zero and the work done equals the change in kinetic energy:
$$\tfrac{1}{2}mv^2 = 13\,600$$
$$\tfrac{1}{2} \times 80 \times v^2 = 13\,600$$
$$v^2 = 340$$
$$v = 18.4\,\text{m s}^{-1}$$

2 (a) The 100N force is the force provided by the cyclist.

(b)

Work done by 100N force $= \begin{bmatrix} 100 \\ 0 \end{bmatrix} \cdot \begin{bmatrix} 50 \\ 0 \end{bmatrix}$
$$= 5000\,\text{J}$$

Work done by normal reaction $= \begin{bmatrix} 0 \\ R \end{bmatrix} \cdot \begin{bmatrix} 50 \\ 0 \end{bmatrix}$
$$= 0$$

Work done by weight $= \begin{bmatrix} -800\cos 80° \\ -800\cos 10° \end{bmatrix} \cdot \begin{bmatrix} 50 \\ 0 \end{bmatrix}$
$$= -6946\,\text{J}$$

$\begin{bmatrix} 0 \\ R \end{bmatrix}$ $\begin{bmatrix} 100 \\ 0 \end{bmatrix}$ $\begin{bmatrix} -800\cos 80° \\ -800\cos 10° \end{bmatrix}$

Total work done = $5000 - 6946 = -1946\,$J

(c) Work done equals change in kinetic energy and so:
$$\tfrac{1}{2}mv^2 - \tfrac{1}{2}mu^2 = -1946$$

Hence the speed is decreasing.

3 (a) $\mathbf{R} = \begin{bmatrix} 0 \\ R \end{bmatrix}$

$\mathbf{W} = \begin{bmatrix} 0 \\ 300 \end{bmatrix}$

(b) Work done by weight $= \begin{bmatrix} 0 \\ 300 \end{bmatrix} \cdot \begin{bmatrix} 80 \\ 0 \end{bmatrix} = 0$

Work done by reaction $= \begin{bmatrix} 0 \\ R \end{bmatrix} \cdot \begin{bmatrix} 80 \\ 0 \end{bmatrix} = 0$

4

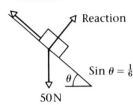

Resistance

Reaction

Sin $\theta = \frac{1}{6}$

50 N

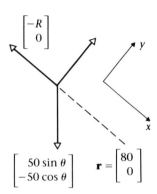

$$\begin{bmatrix} 50 \sin \theta \\ -50 \cos \theta \end{bmatrix} \qquad \mathbf{r} = \begin{bmatrix} 80 \\ 0 \end{bmatrix}$$

Work done by weight $= \begin{bmatrix} 50 \sin \theta \\ -50 \cos \theta \end{bmatrix} \cdot \begin{bmatrix} 80 \\ 0 \end{bmatrix} = 667 \, \text{J}$

Work done by resistance $= \begin{bmatrix} -R \\ 0 \end{bmatrix} \cdot \begin{bmatrix} 80 \\ 0 \end{bmatrix} = -80R \text{ joules}$

Total work done equals change in kinetic energy.
$667 - 80R = \frac{1}{2}mv^2$
$667 - 80R = \frac{1}{2} \times 5 \times 10^2$
$\qquad R = 5.2 \text{ newtons} \quad \text{(to 1 d.p.)}$

5 Initial kinetic energy $= \frac{1}{2} \times 0.01 \times (4^2 + 16^2)$
$\qquad\qquad\qquad\qquad = 1.36$

Final kinetic energy $= \frac{1}{2} \times 0.01 \times (8^2 + 20^2)$
$\qquad\qquad\qquad\qquad = 2.32$

Work done $= 0.96 \, \text{J}$

6

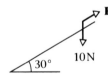

F

10 N

30°

Force down the slope is $10 \cos 60° - F$ newtons
Work done is $(5 - F) \times 5 \text{J}$
Gain in kinetic energy $= \frac{1}{2} \times 1 \times 4^2 - 0$
$\qquad\qquad\qquad\qquad = 8 \text{J}$
$\Rightarrow \quad 25 - 5F = 8$
$\qquad\qquad 5F = 17 \quad \Rightarrow \quad F = 3.4 \text{ newtons}$

7E

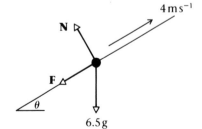

4 m s⁻¹

N

F

θ

6.5 g

Initial KE $= \frac{1}{2} \times 6.5 \times 4^2$ joules
$\qquad\qquad = 52$ joules

$\mu = \frac{2}{3}, \quad \sin \theta = \frac{5}{13}$

(a) Work done by gravity $= -6.5 g \sin \theta \times d$
$\qquad\qquad\qquad\qquad = -6.5 \times 10 \times \frac{5}{13} \times d$
$\qquad\qquad\qquad\qquad = -25d \text{ joules}$

(b) Work done by friction $= -Fd$
Since the block is sliding, $F = \mu N = \frac{2}{3}N$
There is no acceleration perpendicular to the plane,
so $N = 6.5 \text{g} \cos \theta = 65 \times \frac{12}{13} = 60 \text{ newtons}$
Work done by friction $= -\frac{2}{3} \times 60 \times d$
$= -40d \text{ joules}$
Total work done by the forces $= -65d$ joules
The kinetic energy is reduced by 52 joules, and so
$$65d = 52$$
$$d = 0.8 \text{ metres}$$

8E (a)

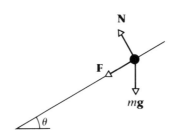

Total work done by friction $= -Fd + -Fd$
$= -2Fd$
Since the body is sliding, $F = \mu N$
There is no acceleration perpendicular to the plane,
So $N = mg \cos \theta$
Total work done by friction $= -2 \mu mgd \cos \theta$

(b)   Work done by gravity $= -mgd \sin \theta$
Work done by the normal contact force $= 0$
Total work done by forces from P to Q $= -mgd \sin \theta - \mu mgd \cos \theta$
$= -mgd (\sin \theta + \mu \cos \theta)$
Work done $=$ change in KE
$-mgd(\sin \theta + \mu \cos \theta) = 0 - \frac{1}{2}mu^2$
$\Rightarrow u = \sqrt{(2gd(\sin \theta + \mu \cos \theta))}$

(c)

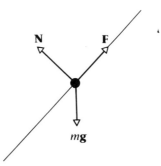

Consider the path from Q to P.
Total work done by the forces $= mgd \sin \theta - \mu mgd \cos \theta$
Let the speed of the body be v.
Then $\frac{1}{2}mv^2 - 0 = mgd \sin \theta - \mu mgd \cos \theta$
$v = \sqrt{(2gd (\sin \theta - \mu \cos \theta))}$

95

3.5 Variable forces

> How can you be sure the maximum speed is reached at point B?
>
> Would taking the more accurate value $g = 9.81\,N\,kg^{-1}$ make a big difference to your answer?
>
> The man's partner (of smaller mass) performs the same manoeuvre. Will her maximum speed be less than the man's?

The work done is $\begin{bmatrix} 0 \\ -700 \end{bmatrix} \cdot \begin{bmatrix} x \\ -y \end{bmatrix} = 700y$

This has a maximum when y is a maximum, i.e. $y = 7$.
If $g = 9.81\,N\,kg^{-1}$

$$\mathbf{w} = \begin{bmatrix} 0 \\ -70 \times 9.81 \end{bmatrix} = \begin{bmatrix} 0 \\ -686.7 \end{bmatrix}$$

$$\begin{bmatrix} 0 \\ -686.7 \end{bmatrix} \cdot \begin{bmatrix} x \\ -7 \end{bmatrix} = \frac{70v^2}{2}$$

$$\Rightarrow \quad 4806.9 = \frac{70v^2}{2}$$

$$\Rightarrow \qquad v = 11.7\,m\,s^{-1}$$

So it does not make a big difference to the answer.

$$\mathbf{w} \cdot \mathbf{r} = \begin{bmatrix} 0 \\ -mg \end{bmatrix} \cdot \begin{bmatrix} x \\ -7 \end{bmatrix} = \frac{mv^2}{2}$$

$$7mg = \frac{mv^2}{2}$$

$$v^2 = 14g$$

$$v = 11.8\,m\,s^{-1}$$

Hence her maximum speed is the same as the man's.

EXERCISE 5

1 (a) $\mathbf{W} = \begin{bmatrix} 0 \\ -400 \end{bmatrix}$ then $\mathbf{W} \cdot \mathbf{r} = \frac{mv^2}{2} - \frac{mu^2}{2}$

$$\begin{bmatrix} 0 \\ -400 \end{bmatrix} \cdot \begin{bmatrix} x \\ -1 \end{bmatrix} = \frac{40v^2}{2} - \frac{40 \times 3^2}{2}$$

$$406 = 20v^2 - 180$$

$$v^2 = 29$$

$$v = 5.4\,m\,s^{-1}\,\text{(to 1 d.p.)}$$

(b) Maximum height occurs when $v = 0$

$$\begin{bmatrix} 0 \\ -400 \end{bmatrix} \cdot \begin{bmatrix} x \\ y \end{bmatrix} = -\frac{mu^2}{2}$$

$$-400y = -\frac{40}{2} \times 3^2$$

$$y = \frac{9}{20} = 0.45 \text{ metre}$$

Hence her maximum height above the ground is $2 + 0.45 = 2.45$ metres.

(c) No, you do not need to know her mass.

$$\begin{bmatrix} 0 \\ -10m \end{bmatrix} \cdot \begin{bmatrix} x \\ y \end{bmatrix} = -\frac{mu^2}{2}$$

$$-10my = -\frac{mu^2}{2} \qquad (m \text{ cancels on each side})$$

$$y = \frac{u^2}{10}$$

2 (a) Assume the scout starts from rest and that $g = 10 \, \text{N kg}^{-1}$. Assume that there is no friction.

$$\mathbf{W} \cdot \mathbf{r} = \frac{mv^2}{2}$$

$$\begin{bmatrix} 0 \\ -mg \end{bmatrix} \cdot \begin{bmatrix} x \\ -8 \end{bmatrix} = \frac{mv^2}{2}$$

$$8mg = \frac{mv^2}{2}$$

$$v^2 = 160$$

$$v = 12.6 \, \text{m s}^{-1}$$

(b) $$\mathbf{W} \cdot \mathbf{r} = \frac{mv^2}{2}$$

$$\begin{bmatrix} 0 \\ -mg \end{bmatrix} \cdot \begin{bmatrix} x \\ -6 \end{bmatrix} = \frac{mv^2}{2}$$

$$6mg = \frac{mv^2}{2}$$

$$v^2 = 120$$

$$v = 11.0 \, \text{m s}^{-1}$$

(c) $11.0 \, \text{m s}^{-1}$ is the same as $\dfrac{11 \times 60 \times 60}{1000} = 39.6 \, \text{km h}^{-1}$

The final speed is too great for the runway to be safe.

3 (a) Displacement of bead $= \begin{bmatrix} 9 \\ 8 \end{bmatrix} - \begin{bmatrix} 6 \\ 7 \end{bmatrix} = \begin{bmatrix} 3 \\ 1 \end{bmatrix}$

The force is $\begin{bmatrix} 2 \\ 5 \end{bmatrix}$.

Work done by the force $= \begin{bmatrix} 3 \\ 1 \end{bmatrix} \cdot \begin{bmatrix} 2 \\ 5 \end{bmatrix}$

$= 6 + 5 = 11$ joules

(b) Work done = change in KE

Initial KE = 0,   final KE = 11

$\frac{1}{2} \times 0.1 \times v^2 = 11$

$v^2 = 220$

$v = 14.8 \, \text{m s}^{-1}$

4 (a) Displacement $= \begin{bmatrix} 10 \\ 12 \end{bmatrix} - \begin{bmatrix} 6 \\ 7 \end{bmatrix} = \begin{bmatrix} 4 \\ 5 \end{bmatrix}$

Work done $= \begin{bmatrix} 4 \\ 5 \end{bmatrix} \cdot \begin{bmatrix} 6 \\ 5 \end{bmatrix}$

$= 24 + 25 = 49$ joules

The change in KE is 49 joules.

(b) The force was not in the direction of motion so the velocity of the ball at A was not parallel to either the force or the displacement.

4 Potential energy

4.1 Gravitational potential energy

> The pencil was stationary before you started to push and it is stationary when you stop pushing, so there is no change in kinetic energy. Does this mean that no work has been done?

As both the normal contact force and the weight are perpendicular to the motion of the pencil, neither do any work and so you should focus on the work done by friction and the work done by the push.

In a simple model of motion you could imagine the pencil going through three distinct stages:

- a (short) period of constant acceleration during which time the force provided by the push is greater than that of friction;

- a period of constant velocity during which time the force provided by the push is equal and opposite to that of friction;

- a (short) period of constant deceleration during which time the force of friction is greater than that provided by the push.

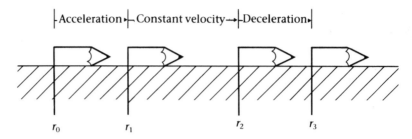

If you take the direction of motion as being positive for the purpose of defining the vectors of force and displacement, then the (displacement, force) graphs will look like this:

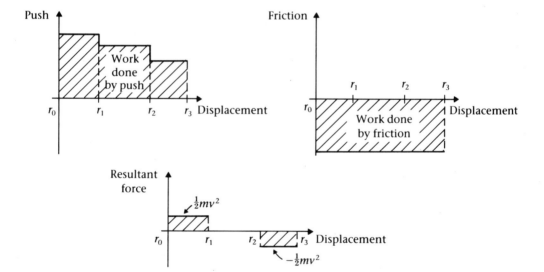

While the force provided by the push does positive work on the pencil, the friction force does negative work because its direction opposes the motion (displacement) of the pencil. Both forces do work, but the net work done on the pencil is zero and hence there is no change in kinetic energy.

> If the pencil has mass m kg and the gravitational force per unit mass is g N kg^{-1}, how much kinetic energy could the pencil acquire if it were dropped through a height of h metres?

The force is mg newtons. The displacement would be h metres in the same direction as the force. The work done would therefore be mgh joules and so the pencil would acquire mgh joules of kinetic energy.

EXERCISE 1

1   The height above the ground is 2 metres.
⇒ gravitational potential energy relative to the ground $= 5 \times 10 \times 2$
$= 100$ joules

2   Height of the child above the ground $= 5 \sin 36°$
$= 2.94$ metres
Gravitational PE relative to the ground $= 30 \times 10 \times 2.94$
$= 882$ joules

3   Let the potential energy at B be zero.
The height of A above B is 7 metres.
Gravitational PE at A relative to B $= 70 \times 10 \times 7$
$= 4900$ joules
Change in PE $= 0 - 4900$
$= -4900$ joules
If the PE is measured relative to a point h metres below B,
PE at A $= 70 \times 10 \times (7 + h)$
PE at B $= 70 \times 10 \times h$
Change in PE $= 700h - 700h - 4900$
$= 4900$ joules

4   (a)

(i) Height of top of ramp $= 34.4 \sin 5°$
$= 3.00$ metres
Work done by gravity $= -500 \times 3.00$
$= -1500$ joules

(ii) Height of top of ramp $= 8.0 \sin 22°$
$= 3.00$ metres
Work done by gravity $= -500 \times 3.00$
$= -1500$ joules

(b) The height the hod is lifted through is the same in each case.

5

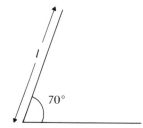

Height of the top of the ladder above the
ground $= l \sin 70°$
Increase in PE $= 50 \times 10 \times l \sin 70°$
But the increase $= 4300$
⇒ $500l \sin 70° = 4300$
$l = 9.15$ metres

4.2   Conserving energy

> Would you obtain the same answer if you found the potential energy
> at each point relative to the level of C?

Yes. The change in potential energy between two points is independent of
your choice of a fixed reference point.

EXERCISE 2

1 (a) PE relative to initial position $= 0.2 \times 3$
$$= 0.6$$

(b) $\qquad$ KE at the start $= \frac{1}{2} \times 0.02 \times 15^2 = 2.25$
PE at the start $= 0$
PE + KE at start = PE + KE after 3 metres
$\Rightarrow \frac{1}{2}mv^2 + 0.6 = 2.25 + 0$
$$v = 12.8\,\text{m s}^{-1}$$

(c) At the highest point of its path, the kinetic energy of the ball is zero.
By conservation of energy:
PE at the highest point $+ 0 = 2.25 + 0$
$$\text{PE} = 2.25 \text{ joules}$$

2

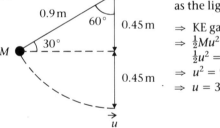

PE at A relative to B $= 0.1 \times 10 \times 1(1 - \cos 80°)$
$$= 0.826 \text{ joule}$$
KE at A $= 0$
But KE + PE at A = KE + PE at B
$\Rightarrow 0.826 + 0 = \frac{1}{2} \times 0.1 \times v^2 + 0$
$$v = 4.07\,\text{m s}^{-1}$$

3 (a)

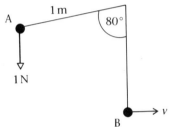

Assume conservation of mechanical energy
as the lighter ball bearing swings down.
$\Rightarrow$ KE gained = PE lost
$\Rightarrow \frac{1}{2}Mu^2 = Mgh$
$\frac{1}{2}u^2 = 10 \times 0.45$
$\Rightarrow u^2 = 9$
$\Rightarrow u = 3\,\text{m s}^{-1}$

(b) The collision is **not** perfectly elastic so you can only assume
conservation of momentum. Mechanical energy is **not** conserved.

Before impact $\qquad\qquad$ **After impact**

The momentum is $3M + 0 = 3Mv$
$$\Rightarrow v = 1\,\text{m s}^{-1}$$

(c) Assume conservation of mechanical energy as the combined mass swings up.

$\Rightarrow$ KE lost = PE gained
$\Rightarrow \frac{1}{2} \times 3M \times 1^2 = 3M \times 10 \times h$
$\Rightarrow h = 0.05$ metre
$\Rightarrow d = 0.85$ metre
$\Rightarrow \theta = \cos^{-1}\left(\dfrac{0.85}{0.9}\right)$

$\qquad = 19°$

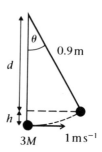

4.3 Elastic potential energy

EXERCISE 3

1 (a) Work done $= \dfrac{kx^2}{2}$

$\qquad\qquad = \dfrac{1000 \times 0.5^2}{2}$

$\qquad\qquad = 125$ joules

(b) Work done $= \dfrac{kx^2}{2}$

$\qquad\qquad = \dfrac{1000 \times 1.5^2}{2}$

$\qquad\qquad = 1125$ joules

2 Let the spring constant be k.

$0.2 = \dfrac{k \times 0.1^2}{2}$

$k = 40\,\mathrm{N\,m^{-1}}$

3 (a) Work done when the spring is compressed 5 cm $= \dfrac{500 \times 0.05^2}{2}$

$\qquad\qquad\qquad\qquad = 0.625$ joules

(b) Work done when the spring is compressed 10 cm $= \dfrac{500 \times 0.1^2}{2}$

$\qquad\qquad\qquad\qquad = 2.5$ joules

So work done to compress the spring a further 5 cm $= 2.5 - 0.625$

$\qquad\qquad\qquad\qquad\qquad\qquad\qquad\qquad = 1.875$ joules

4.4 Conserving mechanical energy

> In what way would the presence of friction affect the motion of the marble?

The presence of friction will mean that not all of the decrease in potential energy will be converted into an increase in kinetic energy. Some of it will be 'lost' to other forms of energy. If the marble slides, mechanical energy will be lost to heat energy and if the marble rolls it will gain 'rotational' kinetic energy as well as 'translational' kinetic energy. Either way, the speed of the marble at the bottom of the chute will be less than expected.

(An object may be stationary in the sense that its centre of mass is stationary. It may, however, still have kinetic energy if it is rotating about an axis through its centre of mass. This form of kinetic energy is looked at in detail in the unit *Modelling with rigid bodies*.)

> Explain why the spring is extended 0.25 m beyond its natural length when the mass is in position B.

The spring constant is $8 \, \text{N m}^{-1}$. This means that a force of 8 N would extend the spring by 1 m, or 1 N extends it by $\frac{1}{8}$ m. Since the mass (0.2 kg) applies a force of 2 N to the spring, the extension is $\frac{2}{8} = 0.25$ m.

EXERCISE 4

1 (a)

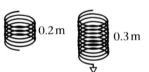

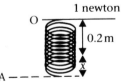

Let the spring constant be k.
$$1 = k \times 0.1$$
$$\Rightarrow k = 10 \, \text{N m}^{-1}$$

Let the gravitational potential energy be measured relative to O.

$$KE = \frac{1}{2}mv^2$$
$$PE = -mg(0.2 + x) = -(0.2 + x)$$
$$EPE = \frac{10 \times x^2}{2}$$

At the point of release:

$$KE = 0 \qquad PE = -1 \times 0.4 \qquad EPE = \frac{10 \times 0.2^2}{2}$$

When the spring is 0.3 metre:

$$KE = \frac{1}{2}mv^2 \qquad PE = -0.3 \qquad EPE = \frac{10 \times 0.1^2}{2}$$

But total mechanical energy is conserved.

$$0 - 0.4 + 0.2 = 0.05v^2 - 0.3 + 0.05$$
$$\Rightarrow 0.05v^2 = 0.05$$
$$v = 1\,\mathrm{m\,s^{-1}}$$

(b) Its elastic potential energy is greatest at the point of release.

2 (a) $T = kx \Rightarrow 20 = 500x$
Its extension is 0.4 metre.

(b) Let the unstretched position be O.
Initial PE $= -2 \times 10 \times 0.1$ Initial KE $= 0$ Initial EPE $= \frac{1}{2} \times 500 \times 0.1^2$
Final PE $= 0$ Final KE $= \frac{1}{2} \times 2 \times v^2$ Final EPE $= 0$
Total mechanical energy is conserved, so:

$$-2 + 0 + 2.5 = 0 + v^2 + 0$$
$$v^2 = 0.5$$
$$v = 0.707\,\mathrm{m\,s^{-1}}$$

3 Let the tension in the string, T newtons, be given by $T = kx$, where x metres is the extension.

$$4 = k \times 0.5 \Rightarrow k = 8$$

KE at B $= 0$ EPE at B $= \frac{1}{2} \times 8 \times 0.5^2$ PE $= 0$
KE at O $= \frac{1}{2}mv^2$ EPE at O $= 0$ (string is unstretched)   PE $= 0$
Total mechanical energy is conserved.
$$\Rightarrow 0 + 1 + 0 = 0.025v^2 + 0 + 0$$
$$\Rightarrow v^2 = 40$$
$$v = 6.32\,\mathrm{m\,s^{-1}}$$
The speed of the mass as it passes O is $6.32\,\mathrm{m\,s^{-1}}$.

4 (a) PE lost by stunt actor $= 76 \times 10 \times 200$
$$= 152\,000\,\mathrm{J}$$

Extension of rope $=$ height $-$ unstretched length
$$= 200 - 100 = 100\,\mathrm{m}$$

Spring constant, $k = 30\,\mathrm{N\,m^{-1}}$

EPE gained by rope $= \dfrac{kx^2}{2}$
$$= \dfrac{30 \times 100^2}{2}$$
$$= 150\,000\,\mathrm{J}$$

(b) The energy of the 'system' is conserved.
Initial (PE + EPE + KE) $=$ Final (PE + EPE + KE)
$$\Rightarrow 152\,000 + 0 + 0 = 0 + 150\,000 + \mathrm{KE}$$
$$\Rightarrow \text{Final KE} = 2000\,\mathrm{J}$$
$$\frac{1}{2}mv^2 = 2000$$
$$\Rightarrow v^2 = \frac{2 \times 2000}{76}$$
$$\Rightarrow v = 7.25\,\mathrm{m\,s^{-1}} \quad \text{(See note (iii).)}$$

Notes   (i) This speed is 'estimated' since the energy conservation equation which was used only dealt with mechanical energy. No account was taken of the energy lost as heat because of friction with the air and internal friction in the rope.

This would reduce the KE remaining, and the final speed slightly.

(ii) The zero level for gravitational PE has been taken as ground level.

(iii) You may like to consider whether a speed of $7.25\,\mathrm{m\,s^{-1}}$ is likely to cause injury. From what height of wall would you have to jump to reach the ground at that speed?

5   Extension = final length − original length

$$= 0.01 - 0.05$$

$$= -0.04 \text{ metre (negative because the spring is compressed)}$$

EPE stored in spring when compressed $= \dfrac{kx^2}{2}$

$$= \dfrac{1000 \times (-0.04)^2}{2}$$

$$= 0.8\,\mathrm{J}$$

The energy of the system is conserved.

Initial (PE + EPE + KE) = Final (PE + EPE + KE)

$$0 + 0.8 + 0 = \text{PE} + 0 + 0$$

$$\text{PE} = mgh = 0.8$$

$$\Rightarrow h = \dfrac{0.8}{0.02 \times 10}$$

Estimated height = 4 metres

NB: KE is zero initially at ground level and zero momentarily at the maximum height reached.

5 Modelling circular motion

5.2 Acceleration

> Would your answer be different if the string was only 0.6 metre long?

No. The answer is independent of the radius of the circle.

EXERCISE 1

1 (a)

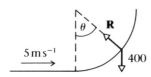

The maximum velocity will occur at the bottom of the bowl.

Assuming no energy is lost and $g = 10\,\mathrm{N\,kg^{-1}}$, the maximum height occurs when $v = 0$.

By conservation of energy:

$$\frac{1}{2}mv^2 - 0 = mgh \quad \text{but } h = 2(1 - \cos\theta)$$

$$\Rightarrow h = \frac{25}{20} = 1.25 \text{ metres}$$

(b) By Newton's second law radially:

$$R - 400\cos\theta = 40a$$

At the highest point, $a = \dfrac{v^2}{r} = 0$

$$\Rightarrow R = 400\cos\theta \text{ where } \cos\theta = 1 - \frac{1.25}{2}$$

$$\Rightarrow R = 150 \text{ newtons}$$

2 (a)

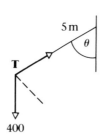

Assume $\cos\theta = \dfrac{4}{5}$ when $v = 0$ and $g = 10\,\mathrm{N\,kg^{-1}}$.
Let the tension in the rope be T newtons and the velocity be $v\,\mathrm{m\,s^{-1}}$.

By Newton's second law radially:

$$T - 400\cos\theta = \frac{40v^2}{5}$$

$$T = \frac{40v^2}{5} + 400\cos\theta \qquad \text{①}$$

By conservation of energy, when $\theta = 0$:

$$\frac{1}{2}mv^2 = mg \times 1 \Rightarrow v^2 = 20 \Rightarrow v = 2\sqrt{5}\,\mathrm{m\,s^{-1}}$$

(b) Substituting in ①:

$$T = \frac{40 \times 20}{5} + 400$$

$$= 560 \text{ newtons at the bottom of the swing}$$

(c) At the top of the swing, $v = 0$ and so $\cos \theta = \dfrac{4}{5}$

$\Rightarrow T = 320$ newtons

3

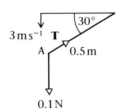

$3\,\text{m s}^{-1}$ **T**

$30°$

A $\quad$ $0.5\,\text{m}$

$0.1\,\text{N}$

Let the velocity at A be $v\,\text{m s}^{-1}$ and take the PE to be zero at the start.

Assume energy is conserved and $g = 10\,\text{N kg}^{-1}$.

(a) $\dfrac{1}{2} \times \cancel{0.01} \times 9 = \dfrac{1}{2} \times \cancel{0.01} + v^2 - \cancel{0.01} \times 10 \times 0.5 \sin 30°$

$\Rightarrow v^2 = 9 + 5$

$= \sqrt{14}\,\text{m s}^{-1}$

(b) By Newton's second law radially:

$$T - 0.1 \cos 60° = \dfrac{mv^2}{0.5}$$

$$T = \dfrac{0.01 \times 14}{0.5} + \dfrac{0.1 \times 1}{2}$$

$$T = 0.33 \text{ newton}$$